EVERYTHING YOU NEED TO KNOW ABOUT

MATH
HOMEWORK

ANNE ZEMAN

KATE KELLY

AN IRVING PLACE PRESS BOOK

SCHOLASTIC REFERENCE

Cover design, Red Herring Design; Cover illustration, Sarajo Frieden
Interior design, Bennett Gewirtz, Gewirtz Graphics, Inc.; Interior illustration, Greg Paprocki

Library of Congress Cataloging-in-Publication Data Available

ISBN 0-439-62522-X

10 9 8 7 6 5 4 3 2 1   05 06 07 08 09

Printed in the U.S.A.
First Printing this Edition, January 2005

Contents

Part 8. Computers and Calculators

Introduction

It's time to do your homework—but you have questions. You need some help, but no adults are around, and you can't reach your classmates on the phone. Where can you go for help?

What Questions Does This Book Answer?

In *Everything You Need to Know About Math Homework*, you will find a wealth of information, including answers to some of the most commonly asked math homework questions, like

- What are prime numbers? You'll find a definition and a list of prime numbers up to 100 on page 7.

- How do you change a base 10 numeral into base 2 or base 5? A table and a step-by-step explanation of converting base 10 to base 2 and 5 is found on pages 19–20.

- How do you do long division? You'll find the procedure explained—with several examples—on page 36.

- How do you find the lowest common denominator of two or more fractions? Look up the answer on page 42.

- How do you reduce fractions to lowest terms? The procedure is explained on page 43.

- How do you calculate percentages, find a number when its percentage is known, or figure out what percent one number is of another? All these calculations are explained, with examples, on pages 50–51.

- How do you round off to the nearest 10, 100, or 1,000? Rounding off is explained on pages 52–53.

- How do you change centimeters to meters or feet to inches? Look at the measurement tables on pages 66–67.

- How do you measure angles? See page 98.

- How do you make a bar graph or a line graph? How do you read graphs that are already made? A complete explanation of creating and reading graphs is found on pages 114–119.

What Is the *Everything You Need to Know About...Homework* series?

The *Everything You Need to Know About...Homework* series is a set of unique reference resources written especially to answer the homework questions of fourth-, fifth-, and sixth-graders. The series provides information to answer commonly asked homework questions in a variety of subjects. Here you'll find facts, charts, definitions, and explanations, complete with examples and illustrations that will supplement schoolwork colorfully, clearly, and comprehensively.

A Note to Parents

It's important to support your children's efforts to do homework. Welcome their questions and see that they have access to a well-lighted desk or table, pencils, paper, and any other books or equipment that they need—such as rulers, calculators, reference books or textbooks, and so on. You might also set aside a special time each day for doing homework, a time when you're available to answer questions that may arise. But don't do your child's homework for them. Remember, homework should create a bond between school and home. It is meant to enhance the lessons taught at school on a daily basis, and to promote good work and study habits. Although it is gratifying to have your children present flawless homework papers, the flawlessness should be a result of your children's explorations and efforts—not your own.

The *Everything You Need to Know About...Homework* series is designed to help your children complete their homework on their own to the best of their abilities. If they're stuck, you can use these books with them to help find answers to troubling homework problems. And remember, when the work is finished, praise your children for a job well done.

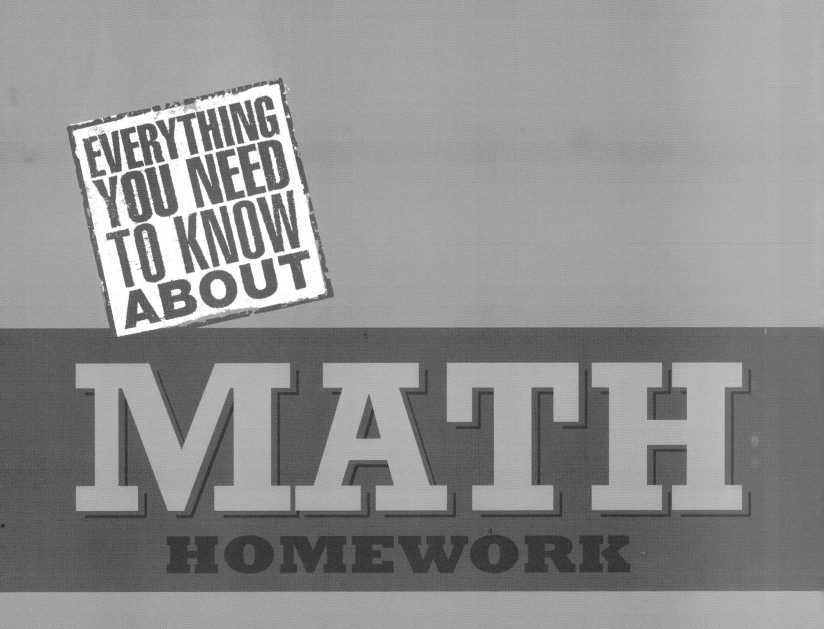

EVERYTHING
YOU NEED
TO KNOW
ABOUT

MATH

HOMEWORK

Chapter 1 — Ancient Number Systems

Who Invented Numbers?

Who invented numbers? No one knows for sure, but the use of numbers may have started as far back as cave people. In order to keep track of tools or skins, a cave person might have matched each tool or skin with a finger. If there were more tools or skins than fingers, the cave person might have picked up pebbles. Each pebble would be used to stand for one tool or skin.

Tally Systems

Matching pebbles to things is one kind of **tally system**. Early tally systems were used to keep track of the days between full moons. This was how our ancestors kept time. The tally system was improved by grouping tally markers in fives—pebbles, lines, etc.

The word **calculate** comes from the Latin word **calculus**, which means "pebble."

Digits to Base 10

Another counting word is **digit**. A digit is any of the numerals from **1** to **9**. The word "digit" is also the name for a finger. So number digits can be counted on finger digits.

The ancient Romans used a counting system that combined **base 5** and **base 10** (see pp.19–20). Our modern system of counting is a base 10 system. Both base 5 and base 10 probably come from counting on fingers. Fingers and hands were among the earliest known calculators!

Most people in the world use a base 10 counting system, and most languages of the world use words for "hand" and "finger" as counting words. The Russian word for "five" is **pyat**, and **pyad** means "hand with fingers spread out." In Persian, "five" is **pantcha** and "hand" is **pentcha**. In Old English, **endleofan**, or eleven, means "ten digits [fingers] with one left over," and **twelf**, or twelve, means "ten digits [fingers] with two left over."

Using Fingers and Toes?

The Mayans, an ancient Central American culture, developed a base 20 counting system. In addition to counting on their fingers, they probably used their toes.

Zero

The Mayans also created a numeral for zero around 500 A.D. So did Hindu astronomers in India. It took the rest of the world about 800 years to catch on to the idea of **zero**, or "nothing."

Writing Numbers

Expressing numbers in written form seems pretty easy.

1 = one
2 = two
10 = ten
100 = one hundred
1,000 = one thousand
10,070 = ten thousand seventy

and so forth.

But, how do you write 136,235 in words? **One hundred thirty-six thousand, two hundred thirty-five** to be exact. So is there a system? You bet.

All "tens" place numbers are written using a hyphen. For example,

21 is **twenty-one**.
63 is **sixty-three**.
97 is **ninety-seven**.

Similarily,

21,000 is **twenty-one thousand**.
63,000 is **sixty-three thousand**.
97,000 is **ninety-seven thousand**.

But what about really big numbers? Write them out as described above, but use commas to separate place values when they are named as you would with numerals (see p. 16). For example,

22,101,003 is written **twenty-two million, one hundred one thousand, three**.

465,080 is written **four hundred sixty-five thousand, eighty**.

2,000,000,010 is written **two billion, ten**.

Number Systems

ARABIC	EGYPTIAN	IONIC & IONIC GREEK	BABYLONIAN	HEBREW	CHINESE	MAYAN	ROMAN
1		A					I
2		B					II
3		Γ					III
4		△					IV
5		E					V
6		F					VI
7		Z					VII
8		H					VIII
9		Θ					IX
10		I					X

3

A Closer Look at Roman Numerals

Roman numerals were created more than 2,000 years ago. They are still used today. You can find Roman numerals on clock and watch faces, on monument and building inscriptions, and on official papers, magazines, and books.

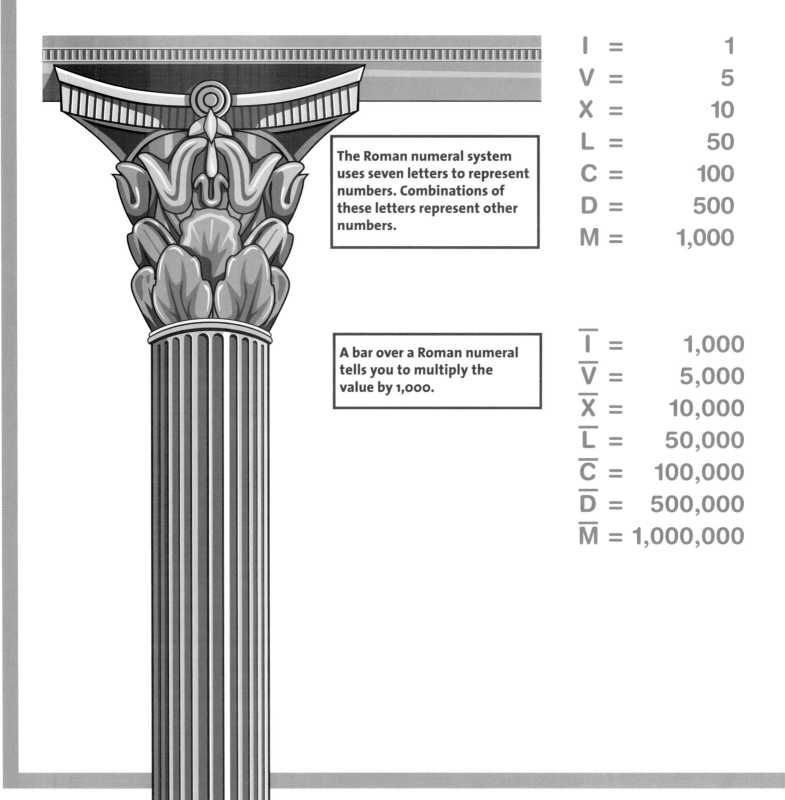

I	=	1
V	=	5
X	=	10
L	=	50
C	=	100
D	=	500
M	=	1,000

The Roman numeral system uses seven letters to represent numbers. Combinations of these letters represent other numbers.

A bar over a Roman numeral tells you to multiply the value by 1,000.

$\overline{I}$	=	1,000
$\overline{V}$	=	5,000
$\overline{X}$	=	10,000
$\overline{L}$	=	50,000
$\overline{C}$	=	100,000
$\overline{D}$	=	500,000
$\overline{M}$	=	1,000,000

Combining Roman Numerals

To make the Roman numeral for 2, I is added to I, so II = 2 (and II + I = III, or 3).

1 = I
2 = I + I or II
3 = I + I + I or III

When a letter representing a number of lesser value appears to the left of a letter of greater value, the lesser value is subtracted from the greater value.

To make the Roman numeral for 4, subtract one from five, or V − I = IV.

4 = V − I or IV
      five minus one   *one less than five*

9 = X − I or IX
      ten minus one   *one less than ten*

40 = L − X or XL
      fifty minus ten   *ten less than fifty*

90 = C − X or XC
      one hundred minus ten   *ten less than one hundred*

"I" may be used before "V" and "X".
"X" may be used before "L" and "C".
"C" may be used before "D" and "M".
For example, 99 is written "XCIX", but not as "IC".

---

1 = I	101 = CI
2 = II	102 = CII
3 = III	103 = CIII
4 = IV	104 = CIV
5 = V	105 = CV
6 = VI	106 = CVI
7 = VII	107 = CVII
8 = VIII	108 = CVIII
9 = IX	109 = CIX
10 = X	110 = CX
11 = XI	120 = CXX
12 = XII	130 = CXXX
13 = XIII	140 = CXL
14 = XIV	150 = CL
15 = XV	160 = CLX
16 = XVI	170 = CLXX
17 = XVII	180 = CLXXX
18 = XVIII	190 = CXC
19 = XIX	200 = CC
20 = XX	300 = CCC
30 = XXX	400 = CD
40 = XL	500 = D
50 = L	600 = DC
60 = LX	700 = DCC
70 = LXX	800 = DCCC
80 = LXXX	900 = CM
90 = XC	1,000 = M
100 = C	

The Decimal System

The **decimal system** uses ten numerals: **0, 1, 2, 3, 4, 5, 6, 7, 8,** and **9**. The word "decimal" comes from the Latin root **decem**, meaning "ten." Within the decimal system are many different kinds of number groupings, called **number sets**. The number sets include: **counting numbers**, **rational numbers**, **prime numbers**, **composite numbers**, **even and odd numbers**, and **integers**.

Arabic into Decimal

The numerals we use today are called **decimal** numerals. These numerals stand for the numbers in the decimal system. The decimal system is also known as the Hindu Arabic system. The decimal system was first created by Hindu astronomers in India more than 1,000 years ago. It spread into Europe around 700 years ago. Here's how the Hindu numerals have changed to become our modern numeral system:

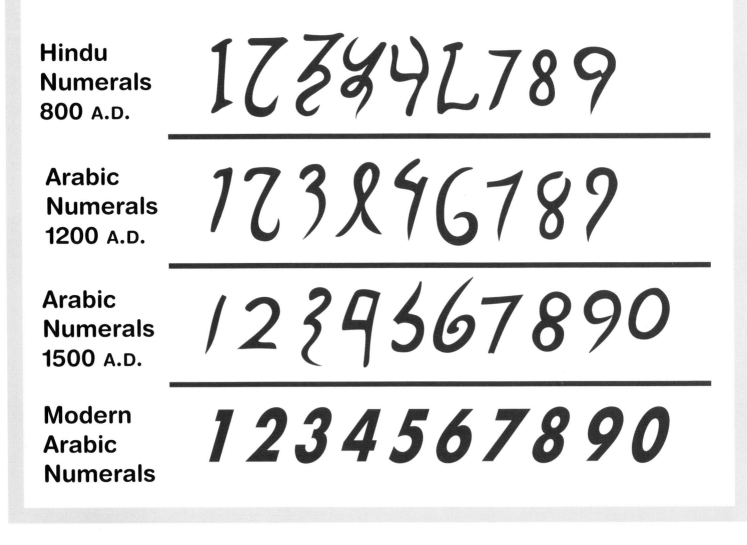

Hindu Numerals 800 A.D.

Arabic Numerals 1200 A.D.

Arabic Numerals 1500 A.D.

Modern Arabic Numerals

Counting Numbers

The set of **counting numbers**, or **natural numbers**, begins with the number **1** and continues into infinity.

{1, 2, 3, 4, 5, 6, 7, 8, 9, 10 . . .}

Whole Numbers

The set of **whole numbers** is the same as the set of counting numbers, except that it begins with **0**.

{0, 1, 2, 3, 4, 5, 6, 7, 8, 9, 10 . . .}

> All counting numbers are whole numbers. Zero is the only whole number that is not a counting number.

Rational Numbers

The set of **rational numbers** includes any number that can be written in the form of a **fraction** (see p. 40), as long as the **denominator** (or bottom part of the fraction) is not equal to **0**.

> All counting numbers and whole numbers can be written as fractions with a denominator equal to 1. That means that all counting numbers and whole numbers are also rational numbers.

Prime Numbers

Prime numbers are counting numbers than can be divided evenly by only two numbers: **1** and themselves. A prime number can also be described as a counting number with exactly two **factors**, **1** and itself (see p. 22). So **1**, because it has only one factor (itself), is not a prime number.

Infinity

The set of counting numbers has no end. It can go on forever. The idea that counting numbers can go on and on is called **infinity**. It has a special symbol:

There is no such thing as the "largest number." You can always add to or multiply a large number to make an even greater number.

$$\infty + 3 = \infty$$

$$\infty \times 10 = \infty$$

If you began writing all the counting numbers today, you could continue writing every moment for every day of the rest of your life and never be finished!

Prime Numbers to 100

2, 3, 5, 7, 11, 13, 17, 19, 23, 29, 31, 37, 41, 43, 47, 53, 59, 61, 67, 71, 73, 79, 83, 89, 97

Fibonacci Numbers

Even nature can be described in numbers. Almost 800 years ago, Italian mathematician Leonardo Fibonacci noticed that there were patterns all around him—in the petals of a flower, the branches of a tree, and the spiral of a snail's shell. In 1202, he discovered a way to describe these patterns through mathematics. He created a number series known today as **Fibonacci numbers**.

The series starts like this:

1, 1, 2, 3, 5, 8, 13, 21, 34, 55, 89, 144 . . .

To create Fibonacci's series of numbers, each number (except for the first **1**) is added to the number to its left. The sum becomes the next number in the series.

1 + 1 = 2,   2 + 1 = 3, 3 + 2 = 5, and so on.

Composite Numbers

Composite numbers are all counting numbers that are not prime numbers. In other words, composite numbers are numbers that have more than two **factors** (see p. 22). The number **1**, because it has only one factor (itself), is **not** a composite number or a prime number.

Composite Numbers to 100

4, 6, 8, 9, 10, 12, 14, 15, 16, 18, 20, 21, 22, 24, 25, 26, 27, 28, 30, 32, 33, 34, 35, 36, 38, 39, 40, 42, 44, 45, 46, 48, 49, 50, 51, 52, 54, 55, 56, 57, 58, 60, 62, 63, 64, 65, 66, 68, 69, 70, 72, 74, 75, 76, 77, 78, 80, 81, 82, 84, 85, 86, 87, 88, 90, 91, 92, 93, 94, 95, 96, 98, 99, 100

Even and Odd Numbers

Even numbers include the numbers **0** and **2** and all numbers that can be divided evenly by **2**. **Odd numbers** are all numbers that cannot be divided evenly by **2**.

Odd and Even Numbers to 100

0 1 2 3 4 5 6 7 8 9 10 11 12 13 14 15 16 17 18 19 20 21 22 23
24 25 26 27 28 29 30 31 32 33 34 35 36 37 38 39 40 41 42
43 44 45 46 47 48 49 50 51 52 53 54 55 56 57 58 59 60 61
62 63 64 65 66 67 68 69 70 71 72 73 74 75 76 77 78 79 80 81
82 83 84 85 86 87 88 89 90 91 92 93 94 95 96 97 98 99 100

Integers

The set of *integers* includes **0**, all of the counting numbers (called **positive** whole numbers), and the whole numbers less than **0** (called **negative** numbers). Integers are shown below on a number line.

> All counting numbers and whole numbers are integers.

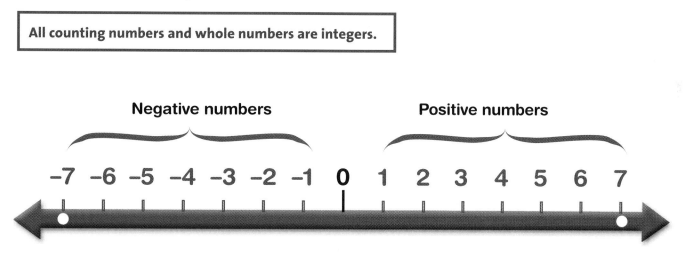

Negative numbers   Positive numbers

–7 –6 –5 –4 –3 –2 –1 0 1 2 3 4 5 6 7

Numbers less than 0 are negative numbers. Numbers greater than 0 are positive numbers.

Note: 0 is neither positive nor negative.

Absolute Value

Absolute value tells the distance of a positive or negative number from **0**. Absolute value is always stated as a positive number.

> The symbol | | means absolute value. For example, $|-3| = 3$ (or the absolute value of -3 is 3) and $|3| = 3$ (or the absolute value of 3 is 3).

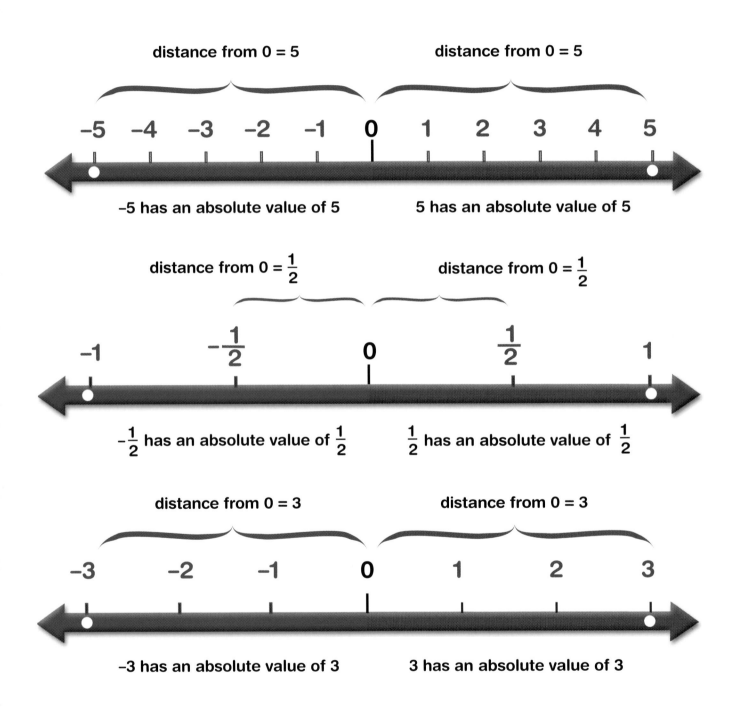

distance from 0 = 5   distance from 0 = 5

–5   –4   –3   –2   –1   0   1   2   3   4   5

–5 has an absolute value of 5   5 has an absolute value of 5

distance from 0 = $\frac{1}{2}$ distance from 0 = $\frac{1}{2}$

–1 $-\frac{1}{2}$ 0 $\frac{1}{2}$ 1

$-\frac{1}{2}$ has an absolute value of $\frac{1}{2}$ $\frac{1}{2}$ has an absolute value of $\frac{1}{2}$

distance from 0 = 3   distance from 0 = 3

–3   –2   –1   0   1   2   3

–3 has an absolute value of 3   3 has an absolute value of 3

What's a Googol?

A googol is the number **1** followed by **100** zeroes.

**10,000,000,000,000,000,000,
000,000,000,000,000,000,000,
000,000,000,000,000,000,000,
000,000,000,000,000,000,000,
000,000,000,000,000,000**

American mathematician Edward Kasner needed to solve a problem using enormous numbers. His nine-year-old nephew, Milton Sirotta, made up the term "googol." Dr. Kasner made up the word "googolplex" to mean **1** followed by a googol of zeros! Googol and googolplex are more simply written in **exponents** (see p. 24). The googolplex is the largest named number.

Bigger Than a Billion

Billion 1,000,000,000

Trillion 1,000,000,000,000

Quadrillion 1,000,000,000,000 ,000

Quintillion 1,000,000,000,000,000,000

Sextillion 1,000,000,000,000,000,000,000

Septillion 1,000,000,000,000,000,000,000,000

Octillion 1,000,000,000,000,000,000,000,000,000

Nonillion 1,000,000,000,000,000,000,000,000,000,000

Decillion 1,000,000,000,000,000,000,000,000,000,000,000

Undecillion 1,000,000,000,000,000,000,000,000,000,000,000,000

Duodecillion 1,000,000,000,000,000,000,000,000,000,000,000,000,000

Tredecillion 1,000,000,000,000,000,000,000,000,000,000,000,000,000,000

Quarthordecillion 1,000,000,000,000,000,000,000,000,000,000,000,000,000,000,000

Qumdecillion 1,000,000,000,000,000,000,000,000,000,000,000,000,000,000,000,000

Sexdecillion 1,000,000,000,000,000,000,000,000,000,000,000,000,000,000,000,000,000

Septdecillion 1,000,000,000,000,000,000,000,000,000,000,000,000,000,000,000,000,000,000

Octodecillion 1,000,000,000,000,000,000,000,000,000,000,000,000,000,000,000,000,000,000,000

Novemdecillion 1,000,000,000,000,000,000,000,000,000,000,000,000,000,000,000,000,000,000,000,000

Vigintillion 1,000,000,000,000,000,000,000,000,000,000,000,000,000,000,000,000,000,000,000,000,000

Googol 10,000,000,000,000,000,000,000,000,000,000,000,000,000,000,000,000,000,000,000,000,000,
000,000,000,000,000,000,000,000,000,000,000,000

Sets

A **set** is a collection of items, for instance: coins, marbles, dishes, trading cards, or even numbers! Items within a set are called **members of the set**. There are three types of sets: equal sets, equivalent sets, and subsets.

Equal sets are sets that have identical members.

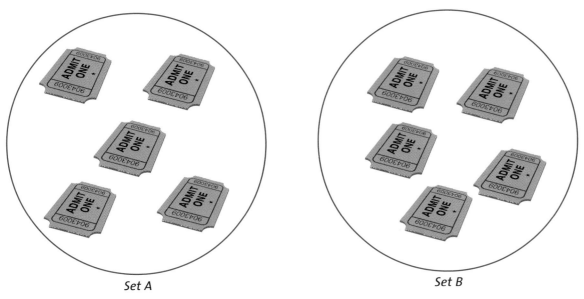

Set A   Set B

Sets A and B are equal sets.

Members Only, Please!

Braces **{ }** are used to show members of a set.

Members of the set of refreshment stand goodies = {popcorn, soda, hot dog, cotton candy}

Equivalent sets are sets that have the same number of members.

Set C   Set D

Sets C and D are equivalent sets.

Subsets are sets contained within other sets.

Set E   Set F

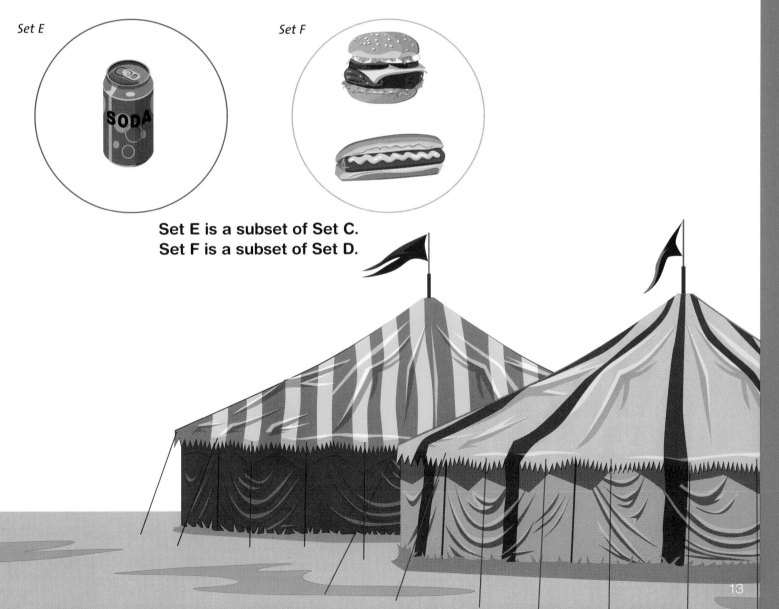

Set E is a subset of Set C.
Set F is a subset of Set D.

∪ means "union of sets."

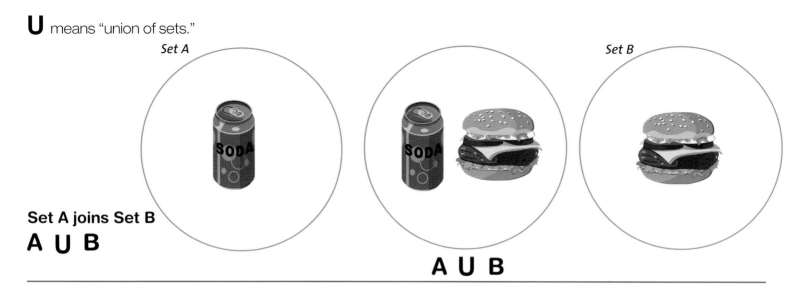

Set A

Set B

Set A joins Set B

A ∪ B

A ∪ B

∩ means "intersection of sets."

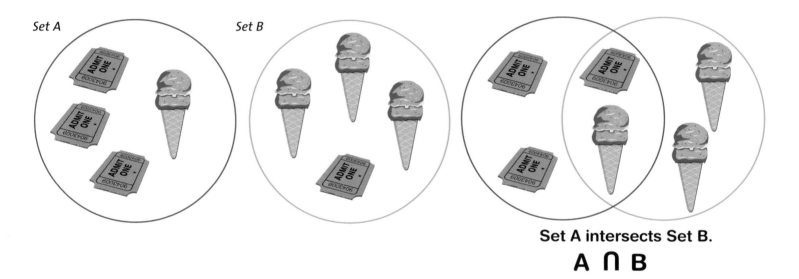

Set A   *Set B*

Set A intersects Set B.

A ∩ B

∈ means "is a member of."

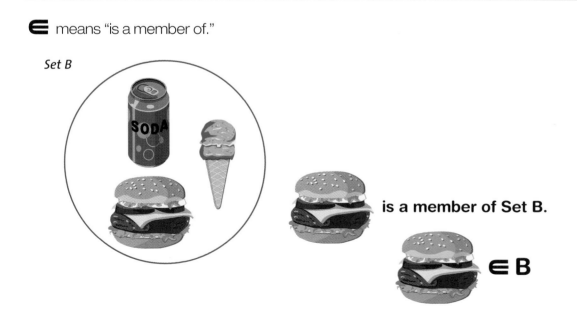

Set B

is a member of Set B.

∈ B

⊂ means "is a proper subset of."

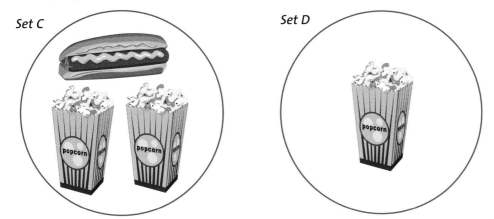

Set C   *Set D*

If all the members of Set D are also members of Set C, but Set C has more members,

D ⊂ C.

⊆ means "is equal to and a subset of."

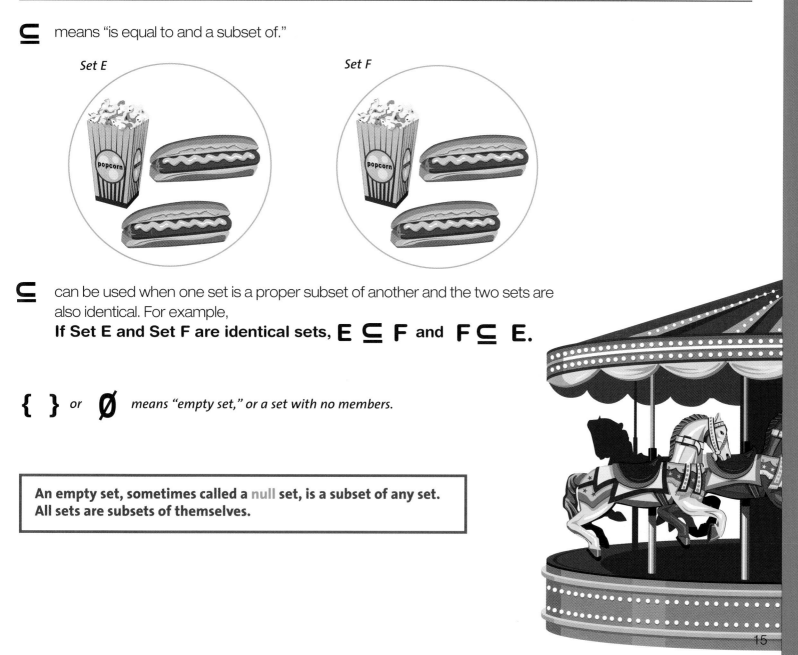

Set E   *Set F*

⊆ can be used when one set is a proper subset of another and the two sets are also identical. For example,

If Set E and Set F are identical sets, E ⊆ F and F ⊆ E.

{ } *or* ∅ *means "empty set," or a set with no members.*

> **An empty set, sometimes called a null set, is a subset of any set. All sets are subsets of themselves.**

Place Value

In the decimal, or base 10, system, numbers are grouped by tens. That means that there are only ten different numerals used to make up decimal numbers:

0, **1**, **2**, **3**, **4**, **5**, **6**, **7**, **8**, and **9**

After these ten numerals are used separately, they are combined to stand for more numbers. (See also Decimals and Place Value, p. 46.)

Ten numerals are used to write all of the numbers in the decimal system.

0	1	2	3	4	5	6	7	8	9
10	11	12	13	14	15	16	17	18	19
20	21	22	23	24	25	26	27	28	29
30	31	32	33	34	35	36	37	38	39
40	41	42	43	44	45	46	47	48	49
50	51	52	53	54	55	56	57	58	59
60	61	62	63	64	65	66	67	68	69
70	71	72	73	74	75	76	77	78	79
80	81	82	83	84	85	86	87	88	89
90	91	92	93	94	95	96	97	98	99

Number: 111

In the number **111**, each numeral **1** means a different number: **one**, **ten**, and **one hundred**. How can the numeral **1** stand for so many numbers? That's called **place value**. The **value** of a numeral depends on what place it's in. If our number system didn't use place value, we would need a lot more than ten numerals—we'd need millions!

hundreds	tens	ones
1	1	1

1 x 100 ←——————— 1 x 10 ←——————— 1 x 1

To read the place value of numerals in a number, read from left to right. Each column has a value 10 times greater than the column to its right.

PERIODS

Three places in the place value chart make up a **period**. Periods are always counted from the right—from the "ones" column—of a number. Periods are separated in numerals by commas.

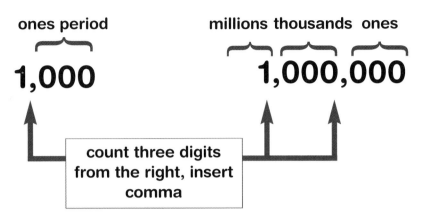

ones period

1,000

millions thousands ones

1,000,000

count three digits from the right, insert comma

Millions Period			Thousands Period			Ones Period		
Hundred Millions	Ten Millions	Millions	Hundred Thousands	Ten Thousands	Thousands	Hundreds	Tens	Ones
100,000,000 900,000,000	10,000,000 90,000,000	1,000,000 9,000,000	100,000 900,000	10,000 90,000	1,000 9,000	100 900	10 90	1 9

PLACE HOLDERS

The numeral **0** is called the **place holder.**

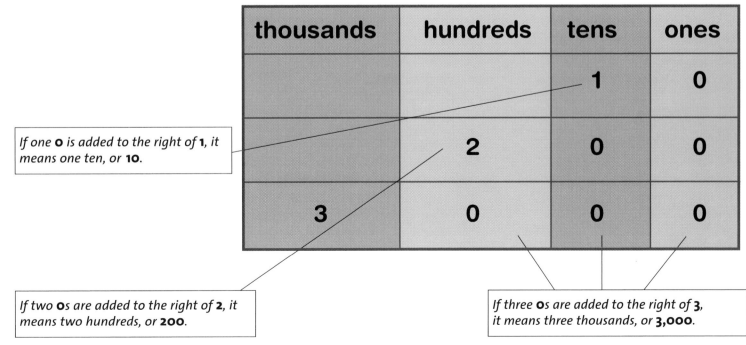

thousands	hundreds	tens	ones
		1	0
	2	0	0
3	0	0	0

*If one **0** is added to the right of **1**, it means one ten, or **10**.*

*If two **0**s are added to the right of **2**, it means two hundreds, or **200**.*

*If three **0**s are added to the right of **3**, it means three thousands, or **3,000**.*

Order

Ordering numbers means listing numbers from least to greatest, or from greatest to least. Two symbols are used in ordering.

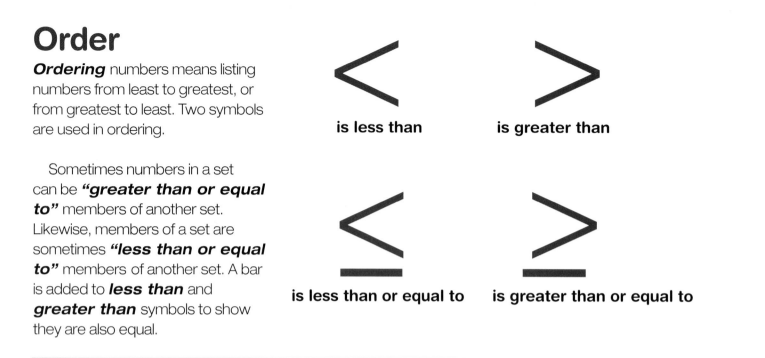

is less than   is greater than

is less than or equal to   is greater than or equal to

Sometimes numbers in a set can be **"greater than or equal to"** members of another set. Likewise, members of a set are sometimes **"less than or equal to"** members of another set. A bar is added to **less than** and **greater than** symbols to show they are also equal.

Number lines show numbers in order. If you follow the number line to the right, the numbers get greater and greater in value. If you follow the number line to the left, the numbers get less and less in value.

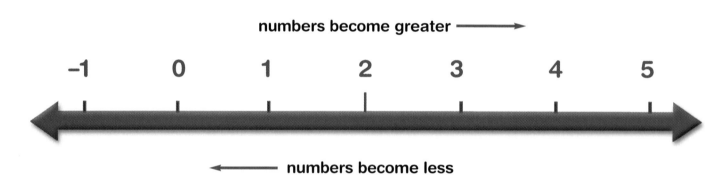

numbers become greater ⟶

−1   0   1   2   3   4   5

⟵ numbers become less

Algebraic or number sentences use the symbols =, ≠, <, >, ≤, or ≥ to show the relationship between two quantities.

Any sentence using the symbol = is called an **equation.**

$4 + 8 = 2 \times 6$
$3x \div 2 = 7$

Any sentence using the symbol ≠, <, >, ≤, or ≥ is called an **inequality**.

$15 > 7$
$6 \neq 3 + 11$
$x + 2 \leq 12$

The symbols < and > were introduced by the English astronomer and mathematician, Thomas Harriot. Harriot was born in 1560 and was educated at Oxford University. He served as a tutor to Sir Walter Raleigh, and was appointed by Raleigh to the office of surveyor with the second expedition to Virginia.

Alternatives to the Decimal System

BASE 2

Base 2, or the binary system, uses only two numerals, **0** and **1**, to represent all the numbers to infinity. Base 2 has place values like base 10, and they look like this:

BASE 5

Base 5 uses five numerals: **0**, **1**, **2**, **3**, and **4**. Like base 2, these numerals are combined to represent numbers to infinity. Base 5's place values look like this:

Decimal (Base 10)	Base 2				
	2^4	2^3	2^2	2^1	2^0
	16	8	4	2	1
0	0	0	0	0	0
1	0	0	0	0	1
2	0	0	0	1	0
3	0	0	0	1	1
4	0	0	1	0	0
5	0	0	1	0	1
6	0	0	1	1	0
7	0	0	1	1	1
8	0	1	0	0	0
9	0	1	0	0	1
10	0	1	0	1	0
⋮	⋮	⋮	⋮	⋮	⋮
15	0	1	1	1	1
16	1	0	0	0	0
⋮	⋮	⋮	⋮	⋮	⋮
20	1	0	1	0	0

Place Value ← →

Base 10 Equivalent ← →

Base 5			
5^3	5^2	5^1	5^0
125	25	5	1
0	0	0	0
0	0	0	1
0	0	0	2
0	0	0	3
0	0	0	4
0	0	1	0
0	0	1	1
0	0	1	2
0	0	1	3
0	0	1	4
0	0	2	0
⋮	⋮	⋮	⋮
0	0	3	0
0	0	3	1
⋮	⋮	⋮	⋮
0	0	4	0

See also Powers and Exponents, p. 24.

CONVERTING BASE 10 TO BASE 2

To change 22 in base 10 to base 2, find the greatest equivalent place value. Look on the conversion chart. It's **20**, or **10100** in base 2. Then continue to find the equivalent value for **2**, or **00010**. Add the columns to find the base 10 / base 2 equivalent.

BASE 10   BASE 2

```
 20   or     1 0 1 0 0 ──── Find the greatest
+12   or    +0 0 0 1 0      equivalent place value.
 22          1 0 1 1 0
```
Find the remaining equivalent place values.

Add columns to find base 10 / base 2 equivalent.

CONVERTING BASE 10 TO BASE 5

To change 18 in base 10 to base 5, find the greatest equivalent place value. It's **16**, or **31** in base 5. Then find the remaining equivalent value. Add the columns to find the base 10 / base 5 equivalent.

BASE 10   BASE 5

```
  16    or      31 ──── Find the greatest
+  2    or    + 02      equivalent place value.
  18            33
```
Find the remaining equivalent place values.

Add columns to find base 10 / base 5 equivalent.

Square, Triangular, and Rectangular Numbers

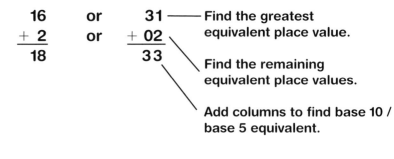

SQUARE NUMBERS

| 1 | 4 | 9 | 16 |

TRIANGULAR NUMBERS

| 1 | 3 | 6 | 10 |

RECTANGULAR NUMBERS

| 1 | 6 | 8 | 12 |

Scientific Notation

When you write a number with more than one digit, the placement of each digit determines its value (see Place Value, p. 16). Look at 12 and 21:

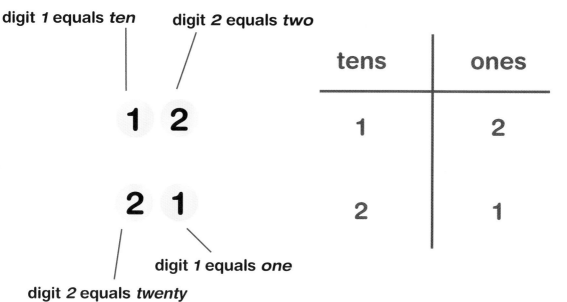

digit 1 equals *ten* **digit 2 equals *two***

tens	ones
1	2
2	1

digit 1 equals *one*

digit 2 equals *twenty*

Using the digits **1** and **2**, you can make the numbers **12** and **21**.

When you write the number **twelve** in numeral form, you ordinarily write **12**. This way of writing a number is known as **standard notation**. But there is another way to write the number twelve:

10 + 2

Or still another way:

(1 x 10) + 2

These spread out, or "expanded" ways of writing **12**, are called **scientific**, or **expanded**, **notation**. You can describe any number using expanded notation. Take a look at the number **six hundred fifty-four thousand, three hundred twenty-one**. In standard notation, this number is written 654,321. In expanded notation, it can be written several ways:

600,000 + 50,000 + 4,000 + 300 + 20 + 1 = 654,321

or

(6 x 100,000) + (5 x 10,000) + (4 x 1,000) + (3 x 100) + (2 x 10) + (1 x 1) = 654,321

or

$6 \times 10^5 + 5 \times 10^4 + 4 \times 10^3 + 3 \times 10^2 + 2 \times 10^1 + 1 = 654{,}321$

> In math, notation means the way numbers are written in numeral form.

Factors and Multiples

FACTORS

Factors are numbers that, when multiplied together, form a new number called a **product** (see Multiplication, p. 33). For example, **1** and **2** are factors of **2**, and **3** and **4** are factors of **12**. Every number except **1** has at least two factors: **1** and itself.

    Composite numbers (see p. 8) have more than two factors. In fact, every composite number can be written as the product of prime numbers. You can see this on a **factor tree**.

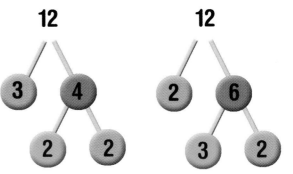

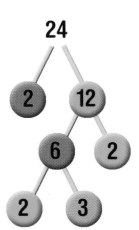

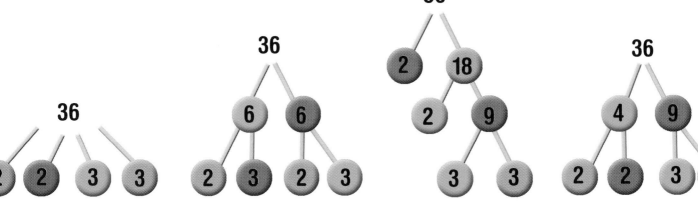

THE GREATEST COMMON FACTOR

Common factors are numbers that are factors of two or more numbers. For example, **2** is a factor of **12** and **36**, which makes **2** a common factor of **12** and **36**. The common factor of two numbers with the greatest value is called the **greatest common factor**. For example, **2**, **3**, **4**, **6**, and **12** are common factors of **12** and **36**, but **12** is the greatest common factor.

MULTIPLES

Find the **multiples** of a whole number by multiplying it by other whole numbers. The multiples of **2**, for example, are:

$$0 \times 2 = \underline{0} \qquad 3 \times 2 = \underline{6}$$
$$1 \times 2 = \underline{2} \qquad 4 \times 2 = \underline{8}$$
$$2 \times 2 = \underline{4} \qquad 5 \times 2 = \underline{10}$$

. . . and so on.

As you can see, the multiples of 2 include **0**, **2**, **4**, **6**, **8**, and **10**. The list continues into infinity!

COMMON MULTIPLES, 0—5

Some numbers share the same multiples. Those multiples are known as **common multiples**.

Number	Multiples					
0	0	0	0	0	0	0
1	0	1	2	3	4	5
2	0	2	4	6	8	10
3	0	3	6	9	12	15
4	0	4	8	12	16	20
5	0	5	10	15	20	25
	0	1	2	3	4	5

The least multiple of two or more numbers is the **least common multiple**. For example, the least common multiple of **2** and **3** is **6**.

$$2 \times 1 = 2 \quad 2 \times 2 = 4 \quad 2 \times 3 = 6$$
$$3 \times 1 = 3 \quad 3 \times 2 = 6$$

The least common multiple is useful in determing the **lowest common denominator** (see p. 42) in fractions. In fact, the lowest common denominator of a fraction is the least common multiple of the numerator and the denominator.

Powers and Exponents

To find the **powers** of a number, multiply the number over and over by itself. The **first power** is the number. The **second power** is the product of the number multiplied once by itself. The **third power** is the number multiplied twice by itself, and so on. For example:

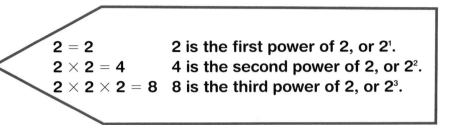

2 = 2   2 is the first power of 2, or 2^1.

2 × 2 = 4   4 is the second power of 2, or 2^2.

2 × 2 × 2 = 8   8 is the third power of 2, or 2^3.

$2^1 = 2 \times 1$ $2^2 = 2 \times 2$ $2^3 = 2 \times 2 \times 2$

$3^1 = 3 \times 1$ $3^2 = 3 \times 3$ $3^3 = 3 \times 3 \times 3$

> There is a special way of writing the power of a number called an exponent. It's the tiny number written above and to the right of the number.

	1	2	3	4	5	6	7	8	9
first power	$1^1 = 1$	$2^1 = 2$	$3^1 = 3$	$4^1 = 4$	$5^1 = 5$	$6^1 = 6$	$7^1 = 7$	$8^1 = 8$	$9^1 = 9$
second power (squared)	$1^2 = 1$	$2^2 = 4$	$3^2 = 9$	$4^2 = 16$	$5^2 = 25$	$6^2 = 36$	$7^2 = 49$	$8^2 = 64$	$9^2 = 81$
third power (cubed)	$1^3 = 1$	$2^3 = 8$	$3^3 = 27$	$4^3 = 64$	$5^3 = 125$	$6^3 = 216$	$7^3 = 343$	$8^3 = 512$	$9^3 = 729$
tenth power	$1^{10} =$ 1	$2^{10} =$ 1,024	$3^{10} =$ 59,049	$4^{10} =$ 1,048,576	$5^{10} =$ 9,765,625	$6^{10} =$ 60,466,176	$7^{10} =$ 282,475,249	$8^{10} =$ 1,073,741,824	$9^{10} =$ 3,486,784,401

EXPONENTS

exponents

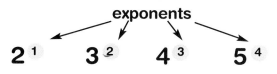

2^1 3^2 4^3 5^4

> Is there a zero power? Yes. Any number, positive or negative, raised to the zero power is equal to 1.

Palindromes

You've probably heard of palindromes in language—words and phrases that are the same read forward or backward.

mom

dad

noon

level

radar

Madam, I'm Adam.

Able was I ere I saw Elba.

A man. A plan. A canal: Panama!

Rats live on no evil star.

There are number palindromes, too. For example:

22

101

2002

45654

You can create your own number palindromes using addition.

First pick a number:

245

Then, reverse its digits to create a new number:

542

Next, add the two numbers:

$$\begin{array}{r} 245 \\ +542 \\ \hline 787 \end{array}$$

You've created a number palindrome!

Sometimes you'll have to keep reversing and adding to create the palindrome.

$$\begin{array}{r} 67 \\ +\ 76 \\ \hline 143 \\ +\ 341 \\ \hline 484 \end{array}$$

Squares and Square Roots

Raising a number to the second power is also called **squaring** a number. For example, **3 squared (3^2)** is equal to **9**, and the **square root** of **9** is **3**.

There is a special way to write the symbol for a square root called a **radical sign**. It looks loke this $\sqrt{}$.

2 squared: $2^2 = 2 \times 2 = 4$

3 squared: $3^2 = 3 \times 3 = 9$

4 squared: $4^2 = 4 \times 4 = 16$

Square root of 16: $\sqrt{16} = 4$

Square root of 9: $\sqrt{9} = 3$

Square root of 4: $\sqrt{4} = 2$

TABLE OF SQUARE ROOTS TO 40

$\sqrt{1}$	1	$\sqrt{121}$	11	$\sqrt{441}$	21	$\sqrt{961}$	31
$\sqrt{4}$	2	$\sqrt{144}$	12	$\sqrt{484}$	22	$\sqrt{1{,}024}$	32
$\sqrt{9}$	3	$\sqrt{169}$	13	$\sqrt{529}$	23	$\sqrt{1{,}089}$	33
$\sqrt{16}$	4	$\sqrt{196}$	14	$\sqrt{576}$	24	$\sqrt{1{,}156}$	34
$\sqrt{25}$	5	$\sqrt{225}$	15	$\sqrt{625}$	25	$\sqrt{1{,}225}$	35
$\sqrt{36}$	6	$\sqrt{256}$	16	$\sqrt{676}$	26	$\sqrt{1{,}296}$	36
$\sqrt{49}$	7	$\sqrt{289}$	17	$\sqrt{729}$	27	$\sqrt{1{,}369}$	37
$\sqrt{64}$	8	$\sqrt{324}$	18	$\sqrt{784}$	28	$\sqrt{1{,}444}$	38
$\sqrt{81}$	9	$\sqrt{361}$	19	$\sqrt{841}$	29	$\sqrt{1{,}521}$	39
$\sqrt{100}$	10	$\sqrt{400}$	20	$\sqrt{900}$	30	$\sqrt{1{,}600}$	40

Why a Square?

We say that **5 squared** equals **25**, and that **25** is a **square number**. Why? Because **25** is the area of a square in which each side equals 5 (see pp. 20 and 74–75).

Basic Math Functions

Chapter 1 Math Symbols

In math, the numerals **0, 1, 2, 3, 4, 5, 6, 7, 8**, and **9** stand for number values. A numeral, then, is a symbol that stands for a number. Numerals aren't the only symbols used in math. Other symbols are used to show how numbers relate to one another. The addition sign, +, for example, is a symbol that stands for "plus." The subtraction sign, –, is a symbol that stands for "minus." So, if you see **3 + 2**, you know **2** will be added together with **3**. And if you see **3 – 2**, you know **2** will be subtracted from **3**.

Basic Math Symbols

+	plus, add	**≤**	is less than or equal to
–	minus, subtract	**:**	is compared to, ratio
×	multiplied by, multiply	**∞**	infinity
÷	divided by, divide	**∠**	angle
=	equal to	**⌐**	right angle
≠	not equal to	**⊥**	perpendicular
>	is greater than	**||**	parallel to
<	is less than	**√**	square root
Ø or { }	empty set	**≈ or ≐**	approximately
| |	absolute value	**::**	proportion sign
≥	is greater than or equal to		

Addition and Subtraction

Combining two or more numbers is called **addition**. The term for addition is **plus**, and the symbol for plus is **+**. The numbers that are combined in addition are called **addends**, and together they form a new number called a **sum**. "Taking away" one or more numbers from another number is called **subtraction**. The term for subtraction is **minus**, and the symbol for minus is **–**. The number being subtracted is called a **subtrahend**. The number being subtracted from is called a **minuend.** The new number left after subtracting is called a **difference** or **remainder**.

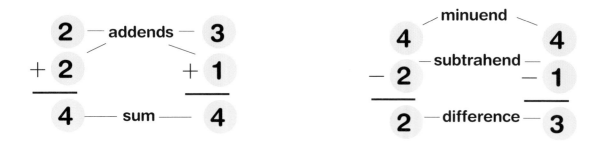

The complete addition or subtraction "sentence" is called an **equation**. An equation has two parts. The two parts are separated by the **equal sign**, =. For example, the **minuend minus the subtrahend equals the difference**. An addition fact or a subtraction fact is the name given to specific addition and subtraction equations.

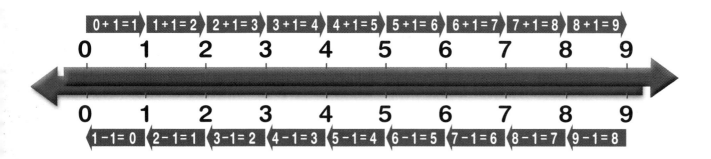

Regrouping Numbers in Addition

Addition often produces sums with a value greater than **9** in a given place (see Place Value, p. 16). The value of ten is then **regrouped** (or **carried**) to the next place.

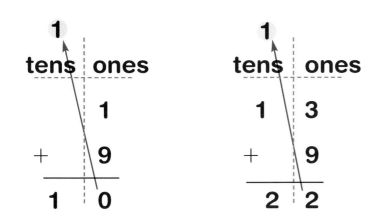

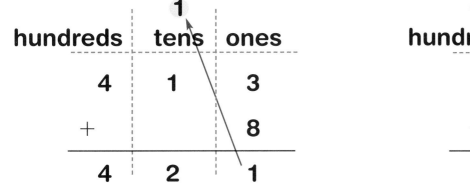

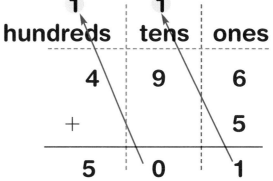

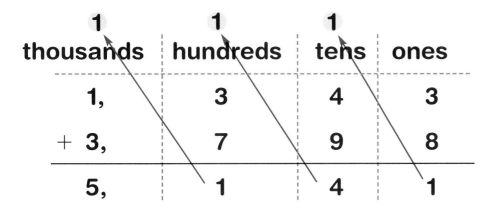

Regrouping in Subtraction

Regrouping, sometimes called *borrowing*, is used when the subtrahend is greater than the minuend in a given place. Regrouping means to take a group of tens from the next greatest place to make a minuend great enough to complete the subtraction process.

	tens	ones
21	1 2→1	1
− 3	−	3
18	1	8

	tens	ones		tens	ones
46	3 4→1	6	3	1	6
− 9		9			9
37	3	7	3	7	

	hundreds	tens	ones
343	3	3 4→1	3
− 9			9
334	3	3	4

	hundreds	tens	ones
521	4 5→11	2→1	1
− 62		6	2
459	4	5	9

	hundreds	tens	ones
506	4 5→9	1 0→1	6
− 8			8
498	4	9	8

Adding and Subtracting Whole Numbers

Adding whole numbers is as simple as 2 + 2! To add two whole numbers, you can simply follow the number line and complete the addition fact.

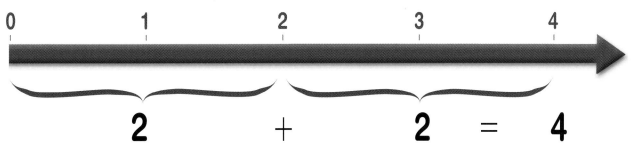

$$2 \quad + \quad 2 \quad = \quad 4$$

Table of Addition Facts

+	1	2	3	4	5	6	7	8	9	10
1	2	3	4	5	6	7	8	9	10	11
2	3	4	5	6	7	8	9	10	11	12
3	4	5	6	7	8	9	10	11	12	13
4	5	6	7	8	9	10	11	12	13	14
5	6	7	8	9	10	11	12	13	14	15
6	7	8	9	10	11	12	13	14	15	16
7	8	9	10	11	12	13	14	15	16	17
8	9	10	11	12	13	14	15	16	17	18
9	10	11	12	13	14	15	16	17	18	19
10	11	12	13	14	15	16	17	18	19	20

The SUM Is Always the SAME

Pick a three-digit number with the first digit greater than the last by at least two. Then reverse the numerals in the number you've picked and subtract this new number from the original number. Next, reverse the numerals in the difference, and add this new number to the difference. The sum will equal 1,089—no matter what number you started with!

$$
\begin{array}{r}
543 \\
-\ 345 \\
\hline
198 \\
+\ 891 \\
\hline
1,089
\end{array}
$$

reverse digits, then subtract from original number

reverse digits, then add to remainder

$$
\begin{array}{r}
614 \\
-\ 416 \\
\hline
198 \\
+\ 891 \\
\hline
1,089
\end{array}
$$

Adding and Subtracting Integers

Adding and subtracting positive integers works the same way as adding and subtracting whole numbers. Adding and subtracting negative numbers works differently.

When you add a negative integer to a positive integer, you are actually subtracting the value of the negative integer from the positive integer.

$$4 + -2 = 4 - 2 = 2$$
$$7 + 3 + -2 = 7 + 3 - 2 = 8$$
$$11 + -6 + 4 + -2 = 11 - 6 + 4 - 2 = 7$$

When you add a negative integer to another negative integer, you add the values of the integers and then add a negative sign in front of them.

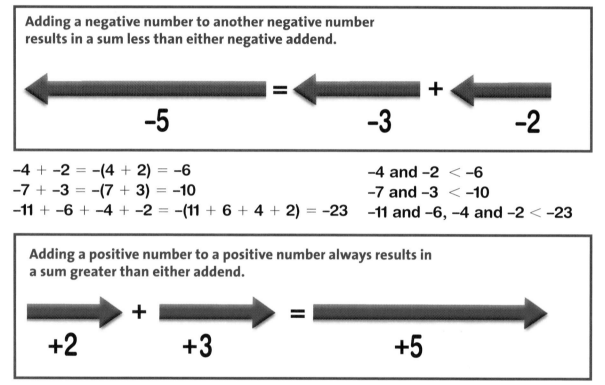

Adding a negative number to another negative number results in a sum less than either negative addend.

$$-5 = -3 + -2$$

$-4 + -2 = -(4 + 2) = -6$	-4 and $-2 < -6$
$-7 + -3 = -(7 + 3) = -10$	-7 and $-3 < -10$
$-11 + -6 + -4 + -2 = -(11 + 6 + 4 + 2) = -23$	-11 and -6, -4 and $-2 < -23$

Adding a positive number to a positive number always results in a sum greater than either addend.

$$+2 + +3 = +5$$

When you subtract a negative integer from a negative integer, you are actually adding a positive integer to the negative integer.

$$-4 - -2 = -4 + 2 = -2$$
$$-7 - -3 - -2 = -7 + 3 + 2 = -2$$
$$-11 - -6 - -4 - -2 = -11 + 6 + 4 + 2 = 1$$

When you subtract a positive integer of greater value from another positive integer, the difference will be a negative integer.

$$2 - 4 = -2$$
$$3 - 7 - 2 = -6$$
$$11 - 6 - 4 - 2 = -1$$

The **Zero Property of Addition** says that the sum of any number and 0 is the number. For example,

$$1 + 0 = 1$$
$$5 + 0 = 5$$
$$10 + 0 = 10, \text{ etc.}$$

Chapter 3 Multiplication and Division

Multiplication

WHAT IS MULTIPLICATION?

Multiplication is a quick form of addition. By multiplying numbers together, you are really adding a series of one number to itself. For example, you can add **2** plus **2**. You can also multiply **2** times **2**. Both **2 plus 2** and **2 times 2** equal **4**.

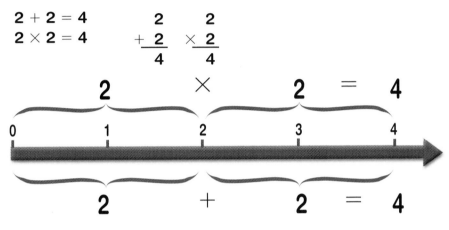

$$2 + 2 = 4$$
$$2 \times 2 = 4$$

But what if you wanted to calculate the number of days in five weeks? You could add **7** days + **7** days + **7** days + **7** days + **7** days, or you could multiply **7** days times **5**. Either way you arrive at **35**, the number of days in five weeks.

$$7 + 7 + 7 + 7 + 7 = 35$$
$$5 \times 7 = 35$$

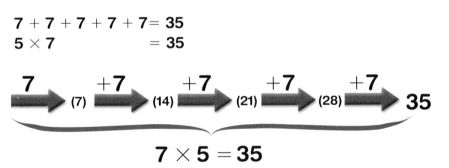

$$7 \times 5 = 35$$

Although multiplication is related to addition, the parts of multiplication are not known as addends. Instead, the parts are known as **multiplicands** and **multipliers**. A multiplication sentence, like an addition sentence, is called an **equation**. But a multiplication sentence results in a **product**, not a sum.

The *multiplicand* and the *multiplier* are *factors* (see p. 22) of the *product*.

33

Multiplication Table

X	0	1	2	3	4	5	6	7	8	9	10	11	12
1	0	1	2	3	4	5	6	7	8	9	10	11	12
2	0	2	4	6	8	10	12	14	16	18	20	22	24
3	0	3	6	9	12	15	18	21	24	27	30	33	36
4	0	4	8	12	16	20	24	28	32	36	40	44	48
5	0	5	10	15	20	25	30	35	40	45	50	55	60
6	0	6	12	18	24	30	36	42	48	54	60	66	72
7	0	7	14	21	28	35	42	49	56	63	70	77	84
8	0	8	16	24	32	40	48	56	64	72	80	88	96
9	0	9	18	27	36	45	54	63	72	81	90	99	108
10	0	10	20	30	40	50	60	70	80	90	100	110	120
11	0	11	22	33	44	55	66	77	88	99	110	121	132
12	0	12	24	36	48	60	72	84	96	108	120	132	144

MULTIPLICATION, STEP-BY-STEP

When the **multiplicand** and the **multiplier** are numbers with two or more digits, multiplication becomes a step-by-step process.

Look at 15 x 3:

```
  1 5
×   3
-----
  1 5
```
First, multiply the ones — 3 x 5. Line up the product with the ones column.

```
  1 5
×   3
-----
  1 5
  3 0
```
Next, multiply the tens — 3 x 1 (ten). Line up the product with the tens column.

Zero is the place holder (see p. 17).

```
  1 5
×   3
-----
  1 5
+ 3 0
-----
  4 5
```
Last, add the ones and tens to find the product of the equation.

Here is a shorter way:

```
  ¹
  1 5
×   3
-----
  4 5
```

First, multiply the ones: 3 x 5 = 15. Put the 5 in the ones column and regroup the 1 to the tens column.

Next, multiply the tens: 3 x 1 = 3.

Last, add the 1 that you regrouped to the 3, and put the sum in the tens column.

Look at 265 x 23:

```
    265    First, multiply           265    Next, multiply by           265   Last, add.
  +  23    the multiplicand        ×  23    the tens — 2 x 5,         ×  23
           by the multiplier                2 x 6, and 2 x 2.
    15      in the ones in            15     Zero is the place           15
   180     the multiplier —          180     holder.               +   180
   600     3 x 5, 3 x 6, and         600                           +   600
           3 x 2.
           Zero is the place          100                          +   100
           holder (see p. 17).      1,200                          + 1,200
                                     4,000                          + 4,000
                                                                     6,095
```

Here is the shorter way:

```
    1 1     First, multiply the ones: 3 x 265
    1 1         3 x 5 = 15 regroup the 1
    265         3 x 6 = 18 plus the regrouped 1 = 19; regroup the 1
  ×  23         3 x 2 =  6 plus the regrouped 1 = 7.
   795
             Next, multiply the tens: 2 x 265
  5300          0 is the place holder
  6,095         2 x 5 = 10 regroup the 1
                2 x 6 = 12 plus the regrouped 1 = 13; regroup the 1
                2 x 2 = 4 plus the regrouped 1 = 5.

             Last, add 795 + 5300 = 6,095.
```

35

Division

WHAT IS DIVISION?

Division is the process of finding out how many times one number, the **divisor**, will fit into another number, the **dividend**. The division sentence results in a **quotient**. The signs of division are ÷, ⌐, and –, and mean **divided by**. You can think of division as a series of repeated subtractions. For example, **40 ÷ 10** could also be solved by subtracting **10** from **40** four times:
40 – 10 – 10 – 10 – 10 = 0.
Because **10** can be subtracted four times, you can say that **40** can be divided by **10** four times, or **40 ÷ 10 = 4**.

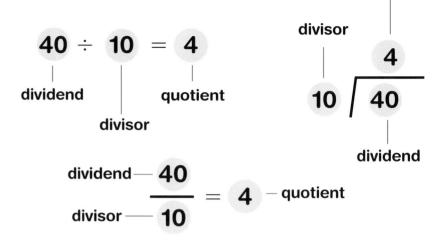

DIVISION, STEP-BY-STEP

Where the dividend and divisor are numbers with two or more digits, division becomes a step-by-step process.

$$\begin{array}{r} 2 \\ 8\overline{)208} \\ -16 \\ \hline 4 \end{array}$$

First, round the divisor up (8 rounds up to 10) and estimate the number of 10s in 20. Answer: 2. Multiply the divisor (8 x 2) and subtract the product from the dividend.

$$\begin{array}{r} 26 \\ 8\overline{)208} \\ -16 \\ \hline 48 \\ -48 \\ \hline 0 \end{array}$$

Next, pull down the next digit from the dividend (8) and repeat the estimation and subtraction process.

$$\begin{array}{r} 26 \\ 8\overline{)208} \\ -16 \\ \hline 48 \\ -48 \\ \hline 0 \end{array}$$

Last, when you can subtract no more, you've found the quotient.

—No remainder

$$\begin{array}{r} 1 \\ 23\overline{)276} \\ -23 \\ \hline 4 \end{array}$$

First, round 23 to 25 and estimate the number of 25s in 27. Answer: 1. Multiply the divisor by 1 (23 x 1) and subtract.

$$\begin{array}{r} 12 \\ 23\overline{)276} \\ -23 \\ \hline 46 \\ -46 \end{array}$$

Next, pull down the next digit from the dividend (6) and repeat the estimation and subtraction process.

$$\begin{array}{r} 12 \\ 23\overline{)276} \\ -23 \\ \hline 46 \\ -46 \\ \hline 0 \end{array}$$

Then, pull down the next digit, estimate, and subtract until you can subtract no more.

—No remainder

Left Behind: Remainders

What happens when numbers don't divide evenly? Many numbers do not fit evenly into other numbers. They are not **evenly divisible** by those numbers, and the leftover number is called the **remainder**.

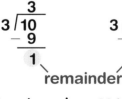

$$\begin{array}{r} 3 \\ 3\overline{)10} \\ -9 \\ \hline 1 \end{array}$$

remainder

10 is not evenly divisible by 3, so 10 ÷ 3 = 3 ¹⁄₁₀ or 3.3.

$$\begin{array}{r} 6 \\ 3\overline{)20} \\ -18 \\ \hline 2 \end{array}$$

20 is not evenly divisible by 3, so 20 ÷ 3 = 6 ⅔ or 6.66.

Remainders can be written as **fractions** (see p. 40). Using the example here, the remainders, 1 and 6, can be expressed as ¹⁄₁₀ and ⅔.
Remainders can also be expressed as **decimals** (see p. 46).

$$\begin{array}{r} 1.5 \\ 8\overline{)12.0} \\ -8 \\ \hline 40 \\ -40 \\ \hline 0 \end{array}$$

$$\begin{array}{r} 2.5 \\ 6\overline{)15.0} \\ -12 \\ \hline 30 \\ -30 \\ \hline 0 \end{array}$$

Whole Numbers

When you multiply whole numbers, the **product** usually has a greater value than either the **multiplicand** or the **multiplier**.

But there are exceptions:
A number multiplied by **1** is always equal to itself.

$$\begin{array}{r} 1 \\ \times\, 1 \\ \hline 1 \end{array} \qquad 21 \times 1 = 21 \qquad \begin{array}{r} 36 \\ \times\, 1 \\ \hline 36 \end{array}$$

A number multiplied by **0** is always equal to **0.**

$$\begin{array}{r} 1 \\ \times\, 0 \\ \hline 0 \end{array} \qquad 21 \times 0 = 0 \qquad \begin{array}{r} 36 \\ \times\, 0 \\ \hline 0 \end{array}$$

To divide whole numbers, reverse the process of multiplication. For example, if **2 x 7 = 14** in a multiplication equation, then in a division equation, **14** is the **dividend** and **7** is the **divisor** with a **quotient** of **2**.

A whole number divided by **1** will always equal itself.

$$1 \div 1 = 1 \qquad 1\overline{)21}^{\,21} \qquad 36 \div 1 = 36$$

Zero divided by a whole number will always equal **0**.

$$0 \div 12 = 0 \qquad 3\overline{)0}^{\,0} \qquad \frac{0}{7} = 0$$

A number cannot be divided by **0**. The answer is **undefined**. (It has no meaning.)

$$12 \div 0 = \text{undefined} \qquad 0\overline{)3}^{\,\text{undefined}} \qquad \frac{7}{0} = \text{undefined}$$

You'll Always Come Up With Nothing

Zero is a special number in multiplication. A number multiplied by **0** always is equal to **0**. This is true for whole numbers, integers, fractions, and decimals.

Multiplicative Identity

The **Identity Property of Multiplication** states that the product of any number and **1** is the number. For example,
$1 \times 1 = 1$, $5 \times 1 = 5$,
$10 \times 1 = 10$, etc.

Integers

Multiplying integers works the same way as multiplying whole numbers, unless one or more of the integers is a negative number. The product of a positive integer multiplied by another positive integer will always be a positive integer. Positive integers may or may not be written with a positive sign: +8 = 8.

$$4 \times 2 = 8 \qquad \begin{array}{r} 3 \\ \times\ 2 \\ \hline 6 \end{array} \qquad \begin{array}{r} 7 \\ \times\ 1 \\ \hline 7 \end{array}$$

The product of a positive integer multiplied by a negative integer will always be a negative integer.

$$4 \times -2 = -8 \qquad \begin{array}{r} 3 \\ \times\ -2 \\ \hline -6 \end{array} \qquad \begin{array}{r} 7 \\ \times\ -1 \\ \hline -7 \end{array}$$

The product of a negative integer multiplied by a positive integer will always be a negative integer.

$$-4 \times 2 = -8 \qquad \begin{array}{r} -3 \\ \times\ 2 \\ \hline -6 \end{array} \qquad \begin{array}{r} -7 \\ \times\ 1 \\ \hline -7 \end{array}$$

The product of a negative integer multiplied by a negative integer will always be a positive integer.

$$-4 \times -2 = 8 \qquad \begin{array}{r} -3 \\ \times\ -2 \\ \hline 6 \end{array} \qquad \begin{array}{r} -7 \\ \times\ -1 \\ \hline 7 \end{array}$$

Remember:
positive x positive = positive
positive x negative = negative
negative x positive = negative
negative x negative = positive

Signed Numbers

Signed numbers are numbers in arithmetic that have a positive (+) or a negative (–) value. When no sign or symbol is present, the number is read as positive. Signed numbers help describe opposite qualities. For example, **30° above zero (+30°)** means something very different than **30° below zero (–30°)**. Or, say you earned 5 dollars for helping with yard work. **$5 earned (+5)**, but you owed your friend 5 dollars for your movie ticket: **$5 owed (–5).**

The rules for adding signed numbers (positive and negative integers) are described on page 32. With multiplication and division, the rules are different.

The **Law of Signs for Multiplication** says that the product of any two numbers that have the same sign (both **+** or **–**) is positive, and that the product of any two numbers that have different signs (one **+** and one **–**) is negative.

$$-1 \times -2 = +2 \qquad\qquad +1 \times -2 = -2$$
$$+1 \times +2 = +2 \qquad\qquad -1 \times +2 = -2$$

If you are multiplying more than two signed numbers, the process works like this:

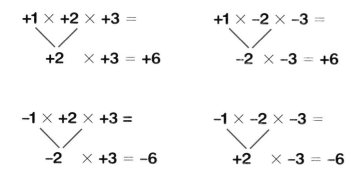

$$+1 \times +2 \times +3 = \qquad\qquad +1 \times -2 \times -3 =$$
$$ +2 \times +3 = +6 \qquad\qquad -2 \times -3 = +6$$

$$-1 \times +2 \times +3 = \qquad\qquad -1 \times -2 \times -3 =$$
$$ -2 \times +3 = -6 \qquad\qquad +2 \times -3 = -6$$

Division of signed numbers works in much the same way as division with positive numbers. However, the sign of the quotient is positive (**+**) if the divisor and the dividend have the same sign. The sign of the quotient is negative (**–**) if the divisor and the dividend have different signs.

$$-2 \div -1 = 2 \qquad\qquad \frac{-2}{-1} = 2$$
$$\text{or} \qquad\qquad\qquad \text{or}$$
$$-2 \div 1 = -2 \qquad\qquad \frac{2}{-1} = -2$$

Fractions

A fraction is a number that represents a part of a whole or a set (see p. 12). The word comes from the Latin word *fractio*, meaning "to break into pieces." In math, a fraction means one or more parts of a whole.

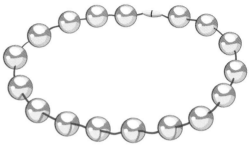

This necklace is made up of beads. Each bead is a member of the "set," or necklace. Since 17 beads make up this necklace, each bead is 1 part of 17 total necklace parts, or 1/17.

A fraction has two parts, a **denominator** and a **numerator**. The denominator is the numeral written under the bar and tells the number of parts a whole is divided into. The numerator is the numeral written above the bar. The numerator tells the number of parts of the whole that are being counted.

$$\frac{\text{numerator}}{\text{denominator}} = \frac{\text{number of parts counted}}{\text{total parts of the whole or set}} = \frac{1}{17}$$

> A fraction is another way of writing a division problem. The fraction 1/4 means 1 ÷ 4. The denominator of a fraction can never be 0 because you cannot divide numbers by 0 (see p. 37).

Proper Fractions

When the numerator of a fraction is less than the denominator, the fraction is called a **proper fraction**.

$$\frac{1}{2} \qquad \frac{2}{5} \qquad \frac{3}{8} \qquad \frac{4}{9} \qquad \frac{5}{11}$$

> The value of a proper fraction is always less than one.

Improper Fractions

When the numerator of a fraction is greater than or equal to the denominator, the fraction is called an *improper fraction*.

$$\frac{3}{2} \qquad \frac{4}{3} \qquad \frac{5}{4} \qquad \frac{6}{5} \qquad \frac{7}{6} \qquad \frac{8}{8}$$

The value of an improper fraction is always greater than or equal to one.

Mixed Numbers

Mixed numbers combine whole numbers and fractions. The values of mixed numbers can also be written as *improper fractions*. To write a mixed number as an improper fraction, multiply the whole number by the denominator of the fraction, and then add the numerator. Use your answer as the new numerator and keep the original denominator.

$$1\frac{1}{2} = \frac{(2 \times 1) + 1}{2} = \frac{3}{2} \qquad\qquad 2\frac{3}{4} = \frac{(4 \times 2) + 3}{4} = \frac{11}{4}$$

To change an improper fraction to a mixed number, divide the numerator by the denominator. Then place the remainder over the old denominator.

$$\frac{3}{2} = 2\overline{)\,3\,} = 1\frac{1}{2} \qquad\qquad \frac{11}{4} = 4\overline{)\,11\,} = 2\frac{3}{4}$$
$$\quad\;\; \underline{-2} \qquad\qquad\qquad\qquad\qquad \underline{-8}$$
$$\quad\;\;\;\; 1 \qquad\qquad\qquad\qquad\qquad\quad 3$$

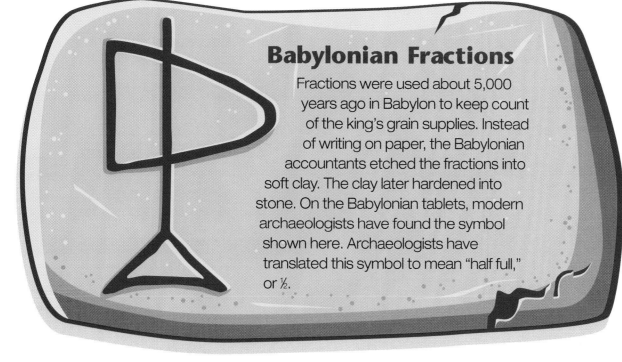

Babylonian Fractions

Fractions were used about 5,000 years ago in Babylon to keep count of the king's grain supplies. Instead of writing on paper, the Babylonian accountants etched the fractions into soft clay. The clay later hardened into stone. On the Babylonian tablets, modern archaeologists have found the symbol shown here. Archaeologists have translated this symbol to mean "half full," or ½.

Common Denominators

Many fractions have **common denominators**. That means that the numbers in their denominators are the same.

$$\frac{1}{2} \qquad \frac{3}{2} \qquad \frac{5}{2}$$

To find common denominators: First, find the **least common multiple** (see p. 23) for the denominators of the fractions you are comparing. Compare:

$\frac{1}{2}$ and $\frac{2}{3}$ Answer: The least common multiple is 6.

Then, divide the common multiple by the denominators.

$$2\overline{)6}^{\,3} \qquad 3\overline{)6}^{\,2}$$

Next, multiply the quotients by the old numerators to calculate the new numerators.

$$\begin{array}{r} 3 \\ \times\,1 \\ \hline 3 \end{array} \qquad \begin{array}{r} 2 \\ \times\,2 \\ \hline 4 \end{array}$$

Last, place the new numerators over the common denominator.

$$\frac{3}{6} \qquad \frac{4}{6}$$

(see p. 23)

EQUIVALENT FRACTIONS

A napkin is folded into two parts. One part is yellow, the other red.

$\frac{1}{2}$ **yellow**

$\frac{1}{2}$ **red**

Then the napkin is folded again. Now there are two yellow parts and two red parts.

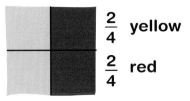

$\frac{2}{4}$ **yellow**

$\frac{2}{4}$ **red**

In this example, the red part of the napkin can be described as ½ red or ¾ red. That makes ½ and ¾ **equivalent fractions.**

When solving math problems, reduce fractions to their lowest equivalent. Rather than describing the napkin as ¾ yellow, call it ½ yellow.

Some Equivalent Fractions

$$\frac{1}{2} = \frac{2}{4} = \frac{3}{6} = \frac{4}{8} = \frac{5}{10}$$

$$\frac{1}{4} = \frac{2}{8} = \frac{3}{12} = \frac{4}{16} = \frac{5}{20}$$

$$\frac{1}{3} = \frac{2}{6} = \frac{3}{9} = \frac{4}{12} = \frac{5}{15}$$

Adding and Subtracting Fractions

To add fractions, the fractions must have **common denominators**. To add fractions with common denominators, simply add the numerators. The sum will become the numerator of your answer. The denominator will remain the same.

$$\frac{1}{3} + \frac{4}{3} = \frac{1+4}{3} = \frac{5}{3}$$

To subtract fractions, you must also find the common denominator. Then subtract the numerators to find the difference. The denominator will remain the same.

$$\frac{7}{8} - \frac{5}{8} = \frac{7-5}{8} = \frac{2}{8}$$

To add or subtract mixed numbers, find a common denominator for the fractional part of the number. Add or subtract the fractions. Then add or subtract the whole numbers. Combine the whole number and the fraction part of answer and reduce if necessary. For example:

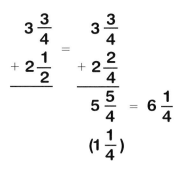

Sometimes when subtracting mixed numbers, it is necessary to regroup in order to subtract the fraction. "Borrow" one whole from the whole number. For example, in the illustration below, one whole is borrowed from the whole number 5 and the fraction is then rewritten as 4 ⁵⁄₄). Write the one whole as a fraction using the **common denominator** of the problem. Add the value of the whole to the fraction in the **minuend** before subtracting.

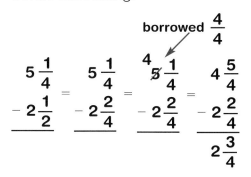

Reducing Fractions to Lowest Terms

Use Greatest Common Factors

To reduce a fraction to its lowest terms, divide both the numerator and the denominator by their **greatest common factor** (p. 22). For example,

$$\frac{4}{8} \div \frac{4}{4} = \frac{1}{2}$$

4 is the greatest common factor of 4 and 8

$$\frac{6}{9} \div \frac{3}{3} = \frac{2}{3}$$

3 is the greatest common factor of 6 and 9

Use Common Prime Factors

To reduce a fraction to its lowest terms, divide both the numerator and the denominator by their **common prime factors**. Then reduce further, if possible, using the greatest common factor (see p.22). For example,

$$\frac{66}{44} \div \frac{11}{11} = \frac{6}{4} \div \frac{2}{2} = \frac{3}{2}$$

11 is the greatest prime factor   *2 is the greatest common factor*

Adding and subtracting fractions is impossible without first writing the fractions with common denominators.

Multiplying and Dividing Fractions

MULTIPLYING

To multiply a fraction by a whole number, change the whole number to a fraction by placing it over a denominator of one. (This does not change the value of the whole number.) Multiply the numerators, then multiply the denominators to get the product.

$$\frac{1}{2} \times 1 = \frac{1}{2} \times \frac{1}{1} = \frac{1 \times 1}{2 \times 1} = \frac{1}{2}$$

$$\frac{2}{7} \times 3 = \frac{2}{7} \times \frac{3}{1} = \frac{2 \times 3}{7 \times 1} = \frac{6}{7}$$

$$\frac{8}{9} \times 6 = \frac{8}{9} \times \frac{6}{1} = \frac{8 \times 6}{9 \times 1} = \frac{48}{9} = 5\frac{3}{9} = 5\frac{1}{3}$$

> **To change improper fractions to mixed numerals, be sure the fraction part of the mixed number is written in the lowest possible terms.**

To multiply one fraction by another fraction, multiply the numerators. Their product will become the new numerator. Next, multiply the denominators. Their product will become the new denominator.

multiply the numerators

$$\frac{1}{2} \times \frac{1}{3} = \frac{1 \times 1}{2 \times 3} = \frac{1}{6}$$

multiply the denominators

$$\frac{7}{8} \times \frac{1}{3} = \frac{7}{24}$$

$$\frac{4}{3} \times \frac{1}{11} = \frac{4 \times 1}{3 \times 11} = \frac{4}{33}$$

To multiply **mixed numbers** (see p. 41) by fractions, change the mixed numbers to improper fractions. Then multiply the fractions.

change the mixed number to an improper fraction

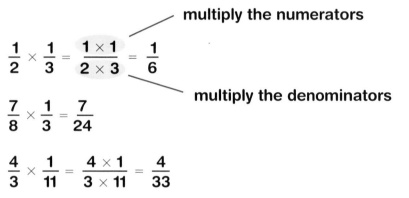

$$1\frac{6}{7} \times \frac{2}{3} = \frac{13}{7} \times \frac{2}{3} = \frac{13 \times 2}{7 \times 3} = \frac{26}{21} = 1\frac{5}{21}$$

change the mixed number to an improper fraction

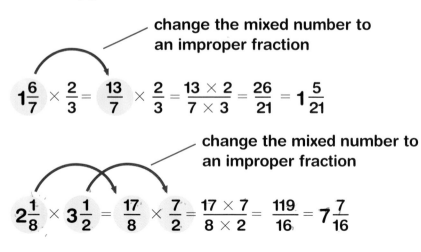

$$2\frac{1}{8} \times 3\frac{1}{2} = \frac{17}{8} \times \frac{7}{2} = \frac{17 \times 7}{8 \times 2} = \frac{119}{16} = 7\frac{7}{16}$$

Canceling and Factoring Out

Canceling and *factoring out* are shortcuts in the multiplication of fractions.

To "cancel," take out **common factors** (p. 22) in the numerator and the denominator before factoring out. For example:

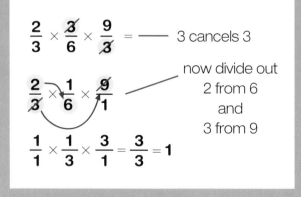

$$\frac{2}{3} \times \frac{3}{6} \times \frac{9}{3} = \underline{} \quad \text{3 cancels 3}$$

now divide out 2 from 6 and 3 from 9

$$\frac{2}{3} \times \frac{1}{6} \times \frac{9}{1}$$

$$\frac{1}{1} \times \frac{1}{3} \times \frac{3}{1} = \frac{3}{3} = 1$$

44

DIVIDING

To divide a fraction by a whole number, change the whole number to an improper fraction with a denominator of one. Invert the divisor fraction to create the reciprocal. Then multiply the fractions.

$$\frac{1}{2} \div 2 = \frac{1}{2} \div \frac{2}{1} = \frac{1}{2} \times \frac{1}{2} = \frac{1}{4} \qquad \frac{2}{7} \div 3 = \frac{2}{7} \div \frac{3}{1} = \frac{2}{7} \times \frac{1}{3} = \frac{2}{21}$$

change whole number to improper fraction

To divide a whole number by a fraction or to divide a fraction by another fraction, **invert** the divisor fraction to create the reciprocal. Then multiply the fractions.

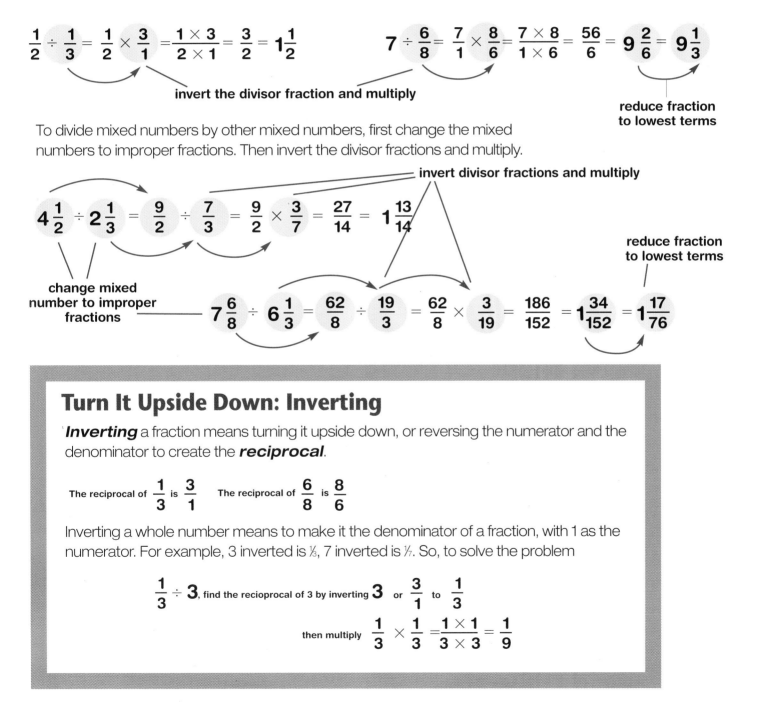

$$\frac{1}{2} \div \frac{1}{3} = \frac{1}{2} \times \frac{3}{1} = \frac{1 \times 3}{2 \times 1} = \frac{3}{2} = 1\frac{1}{2} \qquad 7 \div \frac{6}{8} = \frac{7}{1} \times \frac{8}{6} = \frac{7 \times 8}{1 \times 6} = \frac{56}{6} = 9\frac{2}{6} = 9\frac{1}{3}$$

invert the divisor fraction and multiply

reduce fraction to lowest terms

To divide mixed numbers by other mixed numbers, first change the mixed numbers to improper fractions. Then invert the divisor fractions and multiply.

invert divisor fractions and multiply

$$4\frac{1}{2} \div 2\frac{1}{3} = \frac{9}{2} \div \frac{7}{3} = \frac{9}{2} \times \frac{3}{7} = \frac{27}{14} = 1\frac{13}{14}$$

change mixed number to improper fractions

reduce fraction to lowest terms

$$7\frac{6}{8} \div 6\frac{1}{3} = \frac{62}{8} \div \frac{19}{3} = \frac{62}{8} \times \frac{3}{19} = \frac{186}{152} = 1\frac{34}{152} = 1\frac{17}{76}$$

Turn It Upside Down: Inverting

Inverting a fraction means turning it upside down, or reversing the numerator and the denominator to create the **reciprocal**.

The reciprocal of $\frac{1}{3}$ is $\frac{3}{1}$ The reciprocal of $\frac{6}{8}$ is $\frac{8}{6}$

Inverting a whole number means to make it the denominator of a fraction, with 1 as the numerator. For example, 3 inverted is ⅓, 7 inverted is ⅐. So, to solve the problem

$$\frac{1}{3} \div 3 \text{, find the reciprocal of 3 by inverting } 3 \text{ or } \frac{3}{1} \text{ to } \frac{1}{3}$$

then multiply $\frac{1}{3} \times \frac{1}{3} = \frac{1 \times 1}{3 \times 3} = \frac{1}{9}$

Decimal Fractions and Decimal Numbers

Decimal fractions or **decimals** are fractions with denominators of **10** or powers of **10** (see Powers, p. 24).

10, 100, 1,000, 10,000, and so on

Decimal fractions are written using a decimal point:

$$\frac{1}{10} = .1 \qquad \frac{1}{100} = .01 \qquad \frac{1}{1000} = .001$$

Decimals and Place Value

		hundreds	tens	ones	Decimal point	tenths	hundredths	thousandths
10	$\frac{1}{10}$		1	0	.	1		
205	$\frac{3}{100}$	2	0	5	.	0	3	
4	$\frac{9}{1000}$			4	.	0	0	9

Changing a Fraction to a Decimal

Any fraction can be written as a decimal by dividing the numerator by the denominator, and adding a decimal point in the correct place.

$$\frac{1}{10} = 10\overline{)1.0}^{\,.1} \qquad \frac{3}{5} = 5\overline{)3.0}^{\,.6} \qquad \frac{1}{4} = 4\overline{)1.00}^{\,.25}$$

> In decimal notation, a decimal point distinguishes whole numbers from decimal fractions:
>
> $$1 = 1.0$$
> $$\frac{1}{10} = 0.1$$
> $$1\frac{1}{10} = 1.1$$

Repeating Decimals

Some fractions, when written as a division sentence, never reach a final digit. For example:

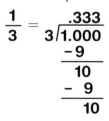

$$\frac{1}{3} = 3\overline{)1.000}^{\,.333}$$

Since the pattern in the quotient repeats, we write ⅓ as .3 or .333 . . . to show that the pattern continues forever.

DECIMAL/FRACTION EQUIVALENTS

halves	fourths	eighths	sixteenths	thirty-seconds	sixty-fourths	
					1	.015625
				1	2	.03125
					3	.046875
		1		2	4	.0625
					5	.078125
				3	6	.09375
					7	.109375
	1		2	4	8	.125
					9	.140625
				5	10	.15625
					11	.171875
			3	6	12	.1875
					13	.203125
				7	14	.21875
					15	.234375
1	2	4	8	16	32	.25
					17	.265625
				9	18	.28125
					19	.296875
			5	10	20	.3125
					21	.328125
				11	22	.34375
					23	.359375
	3		6	12	24	.375
					25	.390625
				13	26	.40625
					27	.421875
			7	14	28	.4375
					29	.453125
				15	30	.46875
					31	.484375
1	2	4	8	16	32	.5

*Example:

halves	fourths	eighths	sixteenths	thirty-seconds	sixty-fourths	
					33	.515625
				17	34	.53125
					35	.546875
			9	18	36	.5625
					37	.578125
				19	38	.59375
					39	.609375
		5	10	20	40	.625
					41	.640625
				21	42	.65625
					43	.671875
			11	22	44	.6875
					45	.703125
				23	46	.71875
					47	.734375
	3	6	12	24	48	.75
					49	.765625
				25	50	.78125
					51	.796875
			13	26	52	.8125
					53	.828125
				27	54	.84375
					55	.859375
		7	14	28	56	.875
					57	.890625
				29	58	.90625
					59	.921875
			15	30	60	.9375
					61	.953125
				31	62	.96875
					63	.984375
2	4	8	16	32	64	1.

*Example: $\dfrac{3}{16} = \dfrac{6}{32} = \dfrac{12}{64} = .1875$

47

Computing with Decimals

Decimals have "common denominators" in the powers of **10**. (See Decimals and Place Value, p. 46.) So, adding and subtracting decimals is easy.

ADDING AND SUBTRACTING DECIMALS

First, align the decimal points of the decimals. Then treat decimal fractions like whole numbers, aligning the decimal point in the sum or difference. Adding and subtracting decimals may look familiar—it's just like adding and subtracting money (see Money, p. 111)!

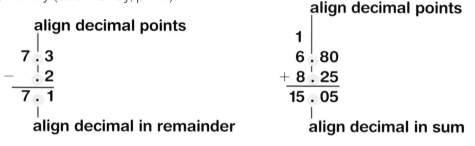

align decimal points

```
    7 . 3
  −   . 2
    7 . 1
```

align decimal in remainder

align decimal points

```
  1
    6 . 80
  + 8 . 25
   15 . 05
```

align decimal in sum

MULTIPLYING DECIMALS

To multiply decimals, treat them as if they were whole numbers, at first ignoring the decimal points.

```
    4.1
  × .3
  1 2 3
```

Next, count the number of places to the right of the decimal point in the multiplicand. Add this to the number of places to the right of the decimal point in the multiplier.

```
  4. 1   multiplicand ←——————— one place
× . 3   multiplier   ←——————— + one place
                                two places
```

Last, insert the decimal point in the product by counting over the appropriate number of places from the right.

```
    4.1
  × .3
  1.2 3     count over two places from the right
```

insert decimal point

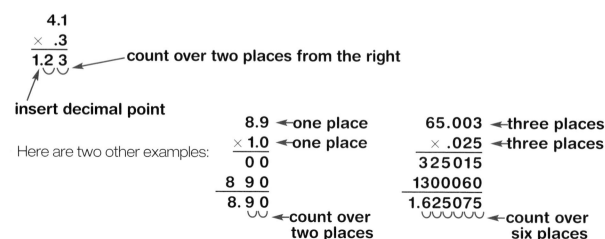

Here are two other examples:

```
     8.9 ←one place
   × 1.0 ←one place
     0 0
   8 9 0
   8.9 0
        ←count over
          two places
```

```
   65.003 ←three places
   × .025 ←three places
   325015
  1300060
  1.625075
          ←count over
            six places
```

Dividing Decimals

Begin dividing decimals the same way you would divide whole numbers.

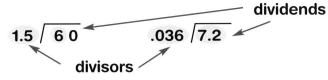

(Note that 6 = 6.0.)

Write the divisor as a whole number. Do this by multiplying the divisor by a power of **10** large enough to make it into a whole number.

$$1.5 \times \textbf{10} = \textbf{15}$$

power of ten

Then multiply the dividend by the same power of 10.

$$6 \times \textbf{10} = \textbf{60}$$

Continue the division process as usual.

align decimal point

$$1\,5. \overline{)6\ 0.}$$
$$\phantom{1\,5. \overline{)}}4.$$

Align the decimal point in the quotient with the decimal point in the dividend.

Here is another example: $.036 \overline{)7.2}$

$$.036 \times \textbf{1,000} = \textbf{36}$$

$$7.2 \times \textbf{1,000} = \textbf{7,200}$$

$$036. \overline{)7\ 200.}$$
$$\phantom{036. \overline{)7}}200.$$

Ratios and Percentages

Ratios describe the size of things in comparison to each other. Ratios are sometimes written in the form of fractions. More often, the symbol **:** is used to separate the numerator and the denominator.

For example, if you ate **2** parts of a pie that had been cut into **5** parts, the ratio of pieces of pie you ate to the uneaten pieces of pie is **2 to 3**. The ratio may be written as **2:3** or ⅔.

If 2 parts of the pie had been eaten, the pie would look like this.

Percentages are ratios written as decimal fractions (see p. 46). The term **percent** means **parts per hundred**. Any fraction with a denominator of **100** can be written as a percentage, using a percent sign, **%**. So, if you ate ⅖ of a pie, you ate **.40** or **40%** of the pie.

$\frac{1}{8}$ or 12.5%
has been eaten

$\frac{3}{4}$ or 75%
has been eaten

$\frac{1}{3}$ or 33.3%
has been eaten

Calculating Ratios and Percentages

CALCULATING EQUAL RATIOS

If one cherry pie is baked for every 4 apple pies, the ratio is 1:4, or ¼.

If the number of apple pies is increased to 12, how many cherry pies are needed to keep the same ratio?

$$\frac{1}{4} = \frac{?}{12}$$ **To find the solution, write the ratios as an equation.**

$$\frac{1}{4} \times \boxed{\frac{3}{3}} = \frac{3}{12}$$ **To solve, multiply (or divide) each term of the first ratio by the same number to make a true statement.**

$$\frac{1}{4} \diagdown \frac{?}{12}$$

$1 \times 12 = 4 \times ?$ **1:4 and 3:12 are equal ratios.**

$$\frac{12}{4} = \frac{4 \times ?}{4}$$ **You can also find the missing term by cross-multiplying and then dividing.**

$3 = ?$

PERCENTAGES

To change a fraction to a percentage, divide the fraction.

$$\frac{2}{5} = 5\overline{)2.00}^{\,.40}$$

Then change the decimal to a fraction with **100** in the denominator, then to a percentage.

$$.40 = \frac{40}{100} = 40\%$$

To change a percentage to a fraction, reverse the process. Be sure to write the fraction in its lowest possible terms (see p. 43).

$$4\% = \frac{4}{100} = \frac{1}{25} \qquad 13\% = \frac{13}{100}$$

To find a percentage of a number, multiply the number by the percentage written in its decimal fraction form. For example, find 25% of 12.

$$.25 \times 12 = 3$$

To find what percentage one number is of another, write the numbers as a fraction. Divide the fraction into its decimal form. Then change the decimal into its percentage form. 12 is what percent of 48?

$$\frac{12}{48} \text{ or } 48\overline{)12.00}^{\,.25} = 25\%$$

To find a number when a percentage of it is known, calculate equal ratios as shown above. For example, nine is 25% of what number?

$$\frac{25}{100} = \frac{9}{?} \qquad 25 \times ? = 100 \times 9$$

$$\frac{25 \times ?}{25} = \frac{900}{25}$$

$$? = 36 \qquad \textbf{Nine is 25\% of 36.}$$

Proportions

A **proportion** is a statement of equality between two ratios. To identify two ratios in proportion, two symbols are used: a double colon (**::**) or an equal sign (**=**). Thus the relationship of

$\frac{1}{3}$ and $\frac{2}{6}$

can be expressed

1:3 :: 2:6 or **1/3 = 2/6**, and is read

1 is to 3 as 2 is to 6
or

$\frac{1}{3}$ is equal to $\frac{2}{6}$.

Rounding and Estimation

What's Rounding?

Rounding means to express a number to the nearest given place. The number in the given place is increased by one if the digit to its right is **5 or greater**. The number in the given place remains the same if the digit to its right is **less than 5**. When rounding whole numbers, the digits to the right of the given place become zeros (digits to the left remain the same). When rounding decimal numbers, the digits to the right of the given place are dropped (digits to the left remain the same).

If you are rounding 3 to the nearest tens place,
you would round down to 0, because 3 is closer to 0 than it is to 10.

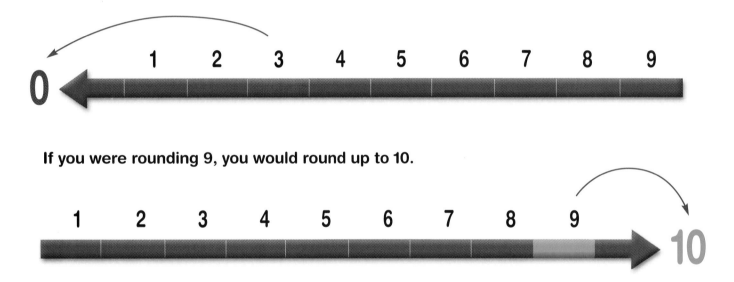

If you were rounding 9, you would round up to 10.

General Rule for Rounding to the Nearest 10, 100, 1,000, and Higher!

Round down from numbers under 5 and round up from numbers 5 and greater.

The same holds true for multiples of 10. Round to the nearest 100 by rounding down from 49 or less and up from 50 or greater. Round to the nearest 1,000 by rounding down from 499 or less and up from 500 or greater.

Why Round?

Sometimes you have to figure out a math problem without using a pencil and paper or a calculator. Rounding numbers makes them easier to work with. Check out the shopping lists. One list tells the prices of five items. The other list shows the same prices, rounded to the nearest ten cents. Which list is easier to add in your head?

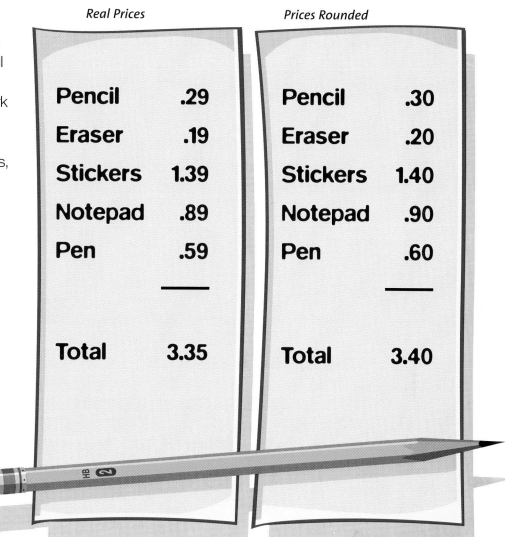

Real Prices

Pencil	.29
Eraser	.19
Stickers	1.39
Notepad	.89
Pen	.59
Total	3.35

Prices Rounded

Pencil	.30
Eraser	.20
Stickers	1.40
Notepad	.90
Pen	.60
Total	3.40

Estimation

To **estimate** means to make an approximate calculation. Rounding allows you to estimate more easily. Here's one way to estimate the sum of **97 + 21**:

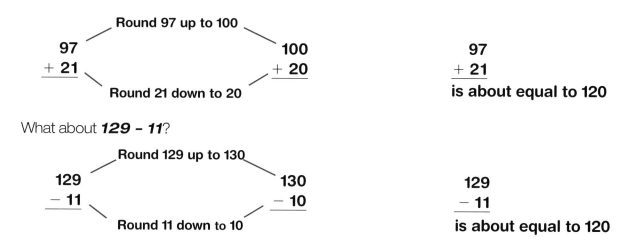

Round 97 up to 100

$$97 + 21$$

Round 21 down to 20

$$100 + 20$$

$$97 + 21$$
is about equal to 120

What about **129 – 11**?

Round 129 up to 130

$$129 - 11$$

Round 11 down to 10

$$130 - 10$$

$$129 - 11$$
is about equal to 120

Chapter 6 Averages and Medians

Averages

The most common way to find an **average** is to add up a list of numbers and divide the sum by the number of items on the list. Another word for average is **mean**.

$$3 + 4 + 6 + 8 + 9 = 30$$

$$30 \div 5 = 6$$

sum ———┘ └——— *number of addends*

So, the average of the numbers **3**, **4**, **6**, **8**, and **9** is **6**.

When do you need to calculate an average? Your grades may be based on the average of all your test scores. In sports, you might want to find out the average height of players on your favorite basketball team.

Anita	60"
Jane	58"
Caitlin	57"
Josie	52"
Tanisha	48"

Medians

Average or **mean** is different from **median**. The median is the middle number in a series of numbers stated in order from least to greatest. An average and a median can be the same number. The average of **3**, **5**, and **7** is **5**:

$$3 + 5 + 7 = 15 \text{ and } 15 \div 3 = 5$$

and the median of **3**, **5**, and **7** is **5**. But average and median are often different numbers. Averages and medians are important in the branches of math called **statistics and probability** (see Statistics and Probability, pages 120–125).

The average height of the players on the court is 55 inches, but the median height among the players is 57 inches—Caitlin's height—because it is the middle number.

Properties and Orders

Addition and multiplication fall under certain rules called **properties** or laws. Among the most important are the **commutative**, **associative**, and **distributive** properties.

Commutative Property

The commutative property of addition says that: **The sum of two or more numbers will always be the same, no matter in what order you add them.**

$2 + 3 = 5$ $6 + 2 = 8$ $153 + 62 = 215$

and   and   and

$3 + 2 = 5$ $2 + 6 = 8$ $62 + 153 = 215$

The commutative property of multiplication says that: **The product of two or more numbers will always be the same, no matter in what order you multiply them.**

$2 \times 3 = 6$ $17 \times 2 = 34$ $153 \times 11 = 1,683$

and   and   and

$3 \times 2 = 6$ $2 \times 17 = 34$ $11 \times 153 = 1,683$

Associative Property

The associative property of addition says that: **No matter how you group a series of numbers, they will always add up to the same sum.**

$(1 + 2) + 3 = 6$

$1 + (2 + 3) = 6$

$(1 + 3) + 2 = 6$

The associative property of multiplication says that: **No matter how you group a series of numbers, they will always multiply to produce the same product.**

$(1 \times 2) \times 3 = 6$

$1 \times (2 \times 3) = 6$

$(1 \times 3) \times 2 = 6$

PARENTHESES IN PROBLEM SOLVING

Parentheses, ( ), are used to group numbers together, especially in long math problems that combine addition, subtraction, multiplication, and division. Always do the operations inside the parentheses first. Then follow the special order for solving long problems called **order of operations** (see p. 57).

$(1 + 2) \times 3 = 3 \times 3 = 9$

$1 + (2 \times 3) = 1 + 6 = 7$

Distributive Property

The distributive property says that: *Multiplication and addition can be linked together by "distributing" the multiplier over the addends in an equation.*

$$3 \times (1 + 4) = 5 = (3 \times 1) + (3 \times 4)$$
$$3 \times 5 = 3 + 12$$
$$15 = 15$$

Here the multiplier is 3, and it is "distributed" to multiply each addend—1 and 4—separately.

Order of Operations

Sometimes the order in which you add, subtract, multiply, and divide is very important. For example, how would you solve the following problem?

$$2 \times 3 + 6$$

Would you group

$$(2 \times 3) + 6 \quad \text{or} \quad 2 \times (3 + 6)?$$

Which comes first, addition or multiplication? Does it matter? Yes. Mathematicians have written two simple steps:

1. **Perform all operations with parentheses and exponents before carrying out the remaining operations in an equation.**
2. **All multiplication and division operations are then carried out, from left to right, in the order they occur.**
3. **Then all addition and subtraction operations are carried out, from left to right, in the order they occur.**

OUTSIDE THE LAW

The commutative and associative properties—or laws—are used only for addition and multiplication. **Subtraction and division are not commutative:**

$$1 - 2 \neq 2 - 1$$
$$-1 \neq 1$$
$$1 \div 2 \neq 2 \div 1$$
$$\frac{1}{2} \neq 2$$

And they are not associative:

$$(1 - 2) - 3 \neq 1 - (2 - 3)$$
$$-1 - 3 \neq 1 - -1$$
$$-4 \neq 2$$
$$(1 \div 2) \div 3 \neq 1 \div (2 \div 3)$$
$$\frac{1}{2} \div 3 \neq 1 \div \frac{2}{3}$$
$$\frac{1}{6} \neq \frac{3}{2}$$

You might say that subtraction and division are "outside the law!"

For example

$$(8 \div 2) + 2 \times 3 - 1$$
$$4 \quad + 2 \times 3 - 1 \qquad \text{Step 1}$$
$$4 \quad + 2 \times 3 - 1$$
$$6 \qquad \text{Step 2}$$
$$4 + 6 - 1$$
$$10 \quad - 1 \qquad \text{Step 2}$$
$$10 \quad - 1 = 9$$

Please Excuse My Dear Aunt Sally

To remember the order of operations, simply remember:
1. Parentheses
2. Exponents
3. Multiplication
4. Division
5. Addition
6. Subtraction, or "Please Excuse My Dear Aunt Sally."

Story Problems

Clue Words

Within every story problem are several **clue words**. These words tell you the kind of math sentence to write to solve the problem.

ADDITION CLUE WORDS

add

sum

total

plus

in all

both

together

increased by

all together

combined

SUBTRACTION CLUE WORDS

subtract

difference

take away

less than

are not

remain

decreased by

have or are left

change
(money problems)

more

fewer

MULTIPLICATION CLUE WORDS

times

product of

multiplied by

by (dimension)

of

DIVISION CLUE WORDS

quotient of

divided by

half [or a fraction]

split

separated

cut up

parts

shared equally

> Division clue words are often the same as subtraction clue words. Divide when you know the total and are asked to find the size or number of "one part" or "each part."

A System for Problem Solving

Following a system of steps can increase your ability to accurately solve problems. Use these steps to solve word problems.

1. Read the problem carefully. Look up the meanings of unfamiliar words.
2. Organize or restate the given information.
3. State what is to be found.
4. Select a strategy (such as making a chart or working backward) and plan the steps to solve the problem.
5. Decide on an approximate answer before solving the problem.
6. Work the steps to solve the problem.
7. Check the final result. Does your answer seem reasonable?

The **Problem Solving System** was used to solve the following problem:

Mary has ten marbles. Lennie has thirteen. How many marbles do they have in all?

1. Mary has ten marbles. Lennie has thirteen. How many marbles do they have in all?

2. Mary—10 marbles
Lennie—13 marbles

3. How many marbles in all?

4. Add

5. A little more than 20 marbles   (10 + 10 = 20)

6.
$$\begin{array}{r} 10 \\ + 13 \\ \hline 23 \end{array} \text{ marbles}$$

7. The final sum of 23 marbles is close to the estimated answer of 20 marbles. The final result is reasonable.

Strategies for Problem Solving

WRITING EQUATIONS FROM SIMPLE STORY PROBLEMS

To write equations for simple story problems:

1. Identify important information. Important information is highlighted below in yellow.

2. Identify what is to be found. The solution—or what is to be found—is highlighted below in blue.

Mary has ten marbles. Lennie has thirteen. How many marbles do they have in all?

Mary has ten marbles.   Lennie has thirteen.   How many marbles do they have in all?

10 + 13 = 23 marbles

Fido has two treats in his bowl. He eats one. How many treats are left?

Fido has two treats in his bowl.   He eats one.   How many treats are left?

2 − 1 = 1 treat

Ian has seven marbles. Kim has three times as many as Ian does. How many marbles does Kim have?

Ian has seven marbles.   Kim has three times as many as Ian does.

How many marbles does Kim have?

7 × 3 = 21 marbles

Mary and Lennie had twenty-three marbles together. They gave one marble to Mustafa. Then Mary and Lennie divided the rest of their marbles into two equal parts. How many marbles does Mary have now?

Mary and Lennie had twenty-three marbles together. They gave one marble to Mustafa.

Then Mary and Lennie divided the rest of their marbles into two equal parts.

How many marbles does Mary have now?

23 − 1 ÷ 2 = 11 marbles

HARDER PROBLEMS

Some story problems are harder to solve than others. For some, you have to write two or three equations to solve the problem. For others, you may need to make charts or lists of information, draw pictures, find a pattern, or even guess and check. Sometimes you have to work backward from a sum, product, difference, or quotient, or simply use your best logical thinking.

Remember!
Not all story problems can be solved in one step. Some require a strategy, or plan, and may take several steps to solve.

LIST/CHART

Marty's library book was six days overdue. The fine is $.05 the first day, $.10 the second, $.20 the third day, and so on. How much does Marty owe?

Marty's library book was six days overdue.   The fine is $.05 the first day, $.10 the second, $.20 the third day, and so on.   How much does Marty owe?

DAYS	1	2	3	4	5	6
FINE	$.05	$.10	$.20	$.40	$.80	$1.60

Answer: $1.60

Veronica, Archie, and Betty are standing in line to buy tickets to a concert. How many different ways can they order themselves in line?

Veronica, Archie, and Betty are standing in line to buy tickets to a concert.

How many different ways can they order themselves in line?

Veronica	Veronica	Archie	Archie	Betty	Betty
Archie	Betty	Veronica	Betty	Veronica	Archie
Betty	Archie	Betty	Veronica	Archie	Veronica

Answer: 6 ways

FIND A PATTERN

Jenny's friend handed her a code and asked her to complete it. The code read 1, 2, 3 Z   4, 5, 6 Y   7, 8, 9 X _____. How did Jenny fill in the blanks?

Jenny's friend handed her a code and asked her to complete it.

The code read 1, 2, 3 Z   4, 5, 6 Y   7, 8, 9 X _____.   How did Jenny fill in the blanks?

Answer: 10, 11, 12 W

DRAW A PICTURE

Mary is older than Jamie. Susan is older than Jamie, but younger than Mary. David is younger than Jamie. Who is oldest?

Mary is older than Jamie.   Susan is older than Jamie,

but younger than Mary.   David is younger than Jamie.

Who is oldest?

Answer: Mary

GUESS AND CHECK

Farmer Joellen keeps cows and chickens in the farmyard. All together, Joellen can count 14 heads and 42 legs. How many cows and how many chickens does Joellen have in the farmyard?

Farmer Joellen keeps cows and chickens in the farmyard.

All together, Joellen can count 14 heads and 42 legs.

How many cows and how many chickens does Joellen

have in the farmyard?

6 cows	Guess a number of cows. Then	6 cows = 24 legs
+ 8 chickens	add the number of chickens to	8 chickens = + 16 legs
14 heads	arrive at the sum of 14 heads. Then	40 legs
	check the total legs.	

7 cows	Adjust your guesses. Then check	7 cows = 28 legs
+ 7 chickens	again until you solve the problem.	7 chickens = + 14 legs
14 heads		42 legs

Answer: 7 cows and 7 chickens

WORK BACKWARD

Marsha was banker for the school play. She took in $175 in ticket sales. She gave Wendy $75 for sets and costumes and Paul $17.75 for advertising and publicity. After paying for the props, Marsha had $32.25 left. How much did the props cost?

Marsha was banker for the school play. She took in $175 in ticket sales. She gave

Wendy $75 for sets and costumes and Paul $17.75 for advertising and publicity.

After paying for the props, Marsha had $32.25 left. How much did the props cost?

```
$ 175.00 tickets          $ 82.25
-   75.00 costumes        -  32.25
$ 100.00                  $ 50.00 cost of props
-   17.75 advertising
$  82.25
```

LOGICAL REASONING

Juan challenged Sheila to guess his grandmother's age in ten questions or fewer. It took her six. Here's what Sheila asked:

Juan challenged Sheila to guess his grandmother's age in ten questions or fewer.

It took her six. Here's what Sheila asked:

"Is she less than fifty?" "No."	50 + years old
"Less than seventy-five?" "Yes."	50 to 74 years old
"Is her age an odd or even number?" "Odd."	ends in 1, 3, 5, 7 or 9
"Is the last number less than or equal to five?" "No."	ends in 7 or 9
"Is it nine?" "No."	ends in 7 — 57 or 67
"Is she in her sixties?" "No."	57 years old

PROBLEM SOLVING, STEP-BY-STEP

Solving some math problems requires several steps and different operations. That means you can make an error in one step that will lead you to an incorrect answer. So, when you're being tested on your problem-solving skills, be sure to:

1. Restate the problem.

2. Show your work.

3. Explain why you did what you did.

4. State your completed answer.

5. On open-ended questions, be sure to label your answers clearly.

Measuring Length and Distance

Chapter 1

A Short History

When people first began measuring, they didn't have rulers, so they used parts of their bodies as guides. For example, in ancient Egypt, the **digit** was a measure based on the average width of an adult finger, about ¾ of an inch.

Digit

Three grains of barley laid end to end equaled one **finger**, and the width of an outstretched adult hand from thumb to pinky tip was called a **span**.

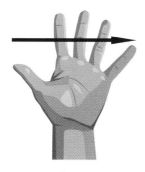

Span

The ancient Egyptians used a measure called the **cubit**. The cubit was the average distance from the elbow to the tip of the middle finger of a grown man. The cubit is used as a measure in the Bible. Noah's Ark was about 300 cubits long. That's about 530 feet.

Cubit

The Egyptians also measured by **paces**. A pace was the distance covered in a single step or stride. The pace was stretched from the heel of the back foot to the big toe of the front foot. Although the pace isn't used for measuring today, we still use the term "pacing off" when we talk about dividing up an area.

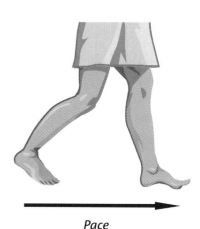

Pace

The Egyptians had a name for a distance of 100 paces—the **stade**. Ancient Greeks called the stade a **stadion**. The Romans called the stade a **stadian**. The stadian was often used as a distance for foot races. From the words **stadion** and **stadian** comes our word **stadium**.

The Romans also created the **mile**. The mile was the distance covered by 1,000 **paces** of a Roman soldier, or about 5,280 feet. Note that a Roman pace, also known as a great pace, is twice the length of an Egyptian pace.

Rod

Copies of the standard yard were made for use all over the country. Soon the length of men's belts were measured from a standard yard of leather or rope. The British created another standard measure, the **rod**. The standard rod measured 16 ½ feet. Before that, the rod was the length covered by the left feet of 16 men, lined up heel to toe.

Fathom

The Vikings probably developed the **fathom**, a distance equal to the span of two outstretched arms. We still use fathoms today to measure the depths of seas and oceans.

The **hand** is another ancient unit of measurement. Today we use hands to measure the height of horses.

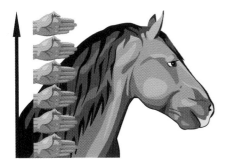

Hands

The Romans were the first to use the **foot** as a measure. The foot was equal to the length of a grown man's foot. Originally, the foot was divided into twelve **uncia**, or inches.

Foot

The Roman measurements—feet, inches, and miles—were picked up by the tribes of Britain. Over time, the measures were changed and some new measurements were created.

During the 12th century, the length of the British king's arm became known as the **yard**. The yard was about three Roman feet long.

Around this same time, the British wanted to make measurements more exact. Using body parts was no longer accurate enough, because two bodies are never exactly the same. So the British created a **standard length** from an iron bar. They called the bar the **standard yard**.

Yard

The U.S. Customary and English Systems

The **U.S. Customary System**, also called the **English System**, is our standard for measuring length. The system is a combination of a number of ancient measures. It is used along with the metric system (see next page).

U.S. CUSTOMARY MEASURES OF LENGTH

Measure	Abbreviation	Equivalent
inch	in.	½ foot
foot	ft.	12 inches
yard	yd.	3 feet (36 inches)
rod	rd.	5 ½ yards
furlong	fur.	40 rods (220 yards)
mile	mi.	1,760 yards (5,280 feet)
league		3 miles (5,280 yards)

Change larger units to smaller units by multiplying

2 yards = ? inches
  2 × 36 (36 inches to a yard) = 72 inches

2 meters = ? cm
  3 × 100 (100 centimeters to a meter) = 300 centimeters

Change smaller units to larger units by dividing

12 feet = ? yards
  12 ÷ 3 (3 feet to a yard) = 4 yards

5,000 meters = ? km
  5,000 ÷ 1,000 meters = 5 km

The Metric System for Measuring Length

In the 1790s, French scientists worked out a system of measurement based on the **meter**. The meter is one ten-millionth of the distance between the north pole and the equator. The French scientists made a metal rod equal to the length of the standard meter.

By the 1980s, the French metal bar was no longer a precise measure for the meter. Scientists figured out a new standard for the meter. They made it equal to the distance traveled by light in a vacuum in $\frac{2}{299,792,458}$ of a second. Since the speed of light in a vacuum never changes, the distance of the meter will not change.

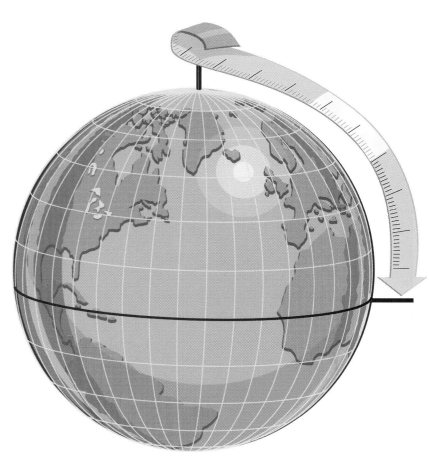

METRIC/U.S. CUSTOMARY LENGTH EQUIVALENTS (ROUNDED)

Metric Unit	Abbreviation	Metric Equivalent	U.S. Equivalent
millimeter	mm	.1 centimeter	.0393 inch
centimeter	cm	10 millimeters	.3937 inch
decimeter	dm	10 centimeters	3.937 inches
meter	m	100 centimeters	39.37 inches
dekameter	dam	10 meters	32.81 feet (10.94 yards)
hectometer	hm	100 meters	109.4 yards
kilometer	km	1000 meters	1,094 yards (.6 mile)

Nautical Measures

Measurement at sea is different from measurement on land. Instead of using miles and kilometers, sailors favor *fathoms* and *nautical miles*.

NAUTICAL MEASURES

Name	Measures	Equivalents
cable	distance	.1 nautical mile
degree	circular distance	60 nautical miles
fathom	depth	6 feet (1.83 meters)
knot	speed	1 nautical mile per hour
mark	depth	fathoms marked on a sounding line
nautical mile	distance	6,076 feet (1,852 meters)
marine league	distance	3 nautical miles (5.6 kilometers)

Space Age Measures

MEASURING EARTH

More than 2,000 years ago, the ancient Greeks worked out a way to measure **circles** and **spheres**. They divided the circle into 360 parts, called **degrees**. The 360 degrees (360°) could also be used to divide spheres. Since the earth is roughly a sphere, the Greeks used degrees (360°) to measure it, too. The Greeks used vertical lines called **longitude** to mark off equal parts of the earth's surface. We still use lines of longitude today.

The line located at **0°** longitude is called the **prime meridian**. Distance is measured east and west of this line. Longitude lines east of the prime meridian are numbered **1°** through **179°**. Longitude lines west of the prime meridian are also numbered **1°** through **179°**. The **180°** line, reached by traveling east or west, is exactly opposite the prime meridian.

The ancient Greeks also drew lines to divide up the earth north and south. These lines are called **lines of latitude**. Latitude is measured from the equator, or **0°**. Latitude lines are numbered from the equator to the North Pole from **0°** through **90°**. Latitude lines are also numbered from **0°** through **90°** from the equator to the South Pole. Degrees of longitude and latitude are further divided into measures called **minutes**. Like minutes in an hour (see p. 87), there are 60 minutes in a degree of longitude or latitude.

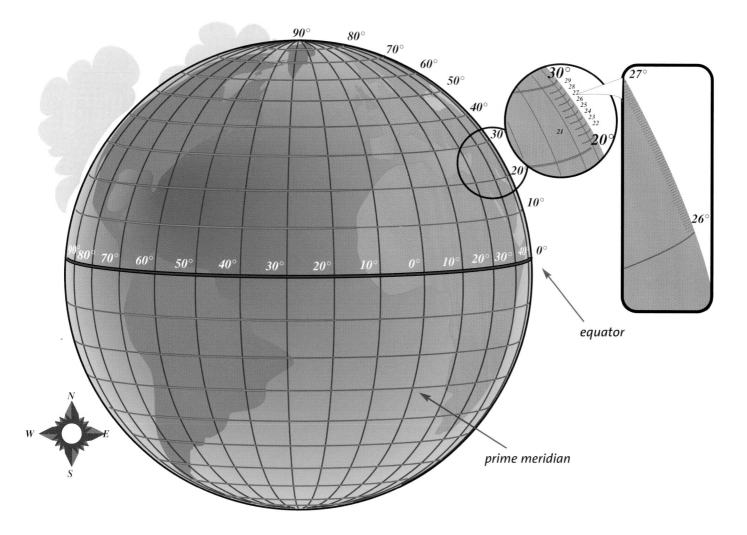

equator

prime meridian

LIGHT-YEARS

The distances in space are too great to be measured easily in miles or kilometers. Instead, scientists use **light-years**. One light-year is the distance light travels in one year. Light travels through space at a speed of 186,282 miles per second, so . . .

1 light-year = 5.878 trillion miles = 9.5 trillion kilometers

Astronomers have also calculated a distance called a **parsec**.

1 parsec = 3.259 light-years

LASER RANGING

Lasers are commonly used today, from grocery store scanning machines to surgical tools. They are also used for measuring distances in space.

In 1969, *Apollo* astronauts left a mirror on the moon. Laser beams bounced off this mirror, allowing us to measure the changes in the distance between the moon and Earth. This technique, called **laser ranging** or LIDAR, is also helping scientists to measure the movements of the continents.

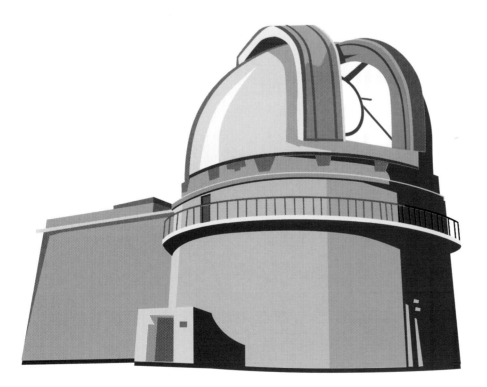

Astronomical Units

Scientists created the **astronomical unit (AU)** to calculate distances within our solar system. The distance from the earth to the sun is 92.9 million miles, or **1** astronomical unit.

AVERAGE DISTANCES OF PLANETS FROM THE SUN IN ASTRONOMICAL UNITS

Mercury	.38 AU
Venus	.72 AU
Earth	1 AU
Mars	1.5 AU
Jupiter	5.2 AU
Saturn	9.6 AU
Uranus	19.2 AU
Neptune	30.1 AU
Pluto	39.4 AU

Chapter 2 Measuring Weight

A Short History

More than 3,000 years ago, the Egyptians invented a scale made of a stick hung from a piece of rope. From the ends of the stick were hung two more ropes. Objects to be weighed were tied to one of the ropes hanging from the end of the stick. Standard weights were tied to the other end. Standard weights included full bags of grain, stones, or seeds.

Egyptian scale

The Weigh We Were

One of the earliest known measures of weight is the Babylonian *mina*. The mina weighed about 21 ounces, about a pound and a half. A five-mina weight was made out of metal and formed into the shape of a duck. A 30-mina weight was formed into the shape of a swan. These weights were placed on scales and used mostly to measure grain.

Another early weight was the Greek *talent*. The talent weighed about 56.9 pounds. The *carat*, known then as the *karob*, meaning "little bean," was equal to the weight of 4 grains of wheat. Carats today equal 3.086 grains and are used to measure precious stones (see Troy Weight, p. 72).

U.S. Customary and English Weights

In the United States, we use three different scales to measure weight: *avoirdupois weight*, *troy weight*, and *apothecaries' measures*.

AVOIRDUPOIS WEIGHT

Avoirdupois weight is used to measure everything except precious metals and gemstones, and medicine.

1 grain (gr.) = 0.002285 ounces

1 dram (dr.) = 27.34 grains

1 ounce (oz.) = 16 drams, or 437.5 grains

1 pound (lb.) = 7,000 grains, or 16 ounces

1 hundredweight (cwt.) = 100 pounds

1 ton = 2,000 pounds, or 20 hundredweights

1 long hundredweight = 112 pounds

1 long ton, or gross = 2,240 pounds or 20 long hundredweights

TROY WEIGHT

Troy weight is used to measure precious metals and gemstones.

1 grain (gr.) = 0.002083 ounces

1 carat (c.) = 3.086 grains

1 pennyweight (dwt.) = 24 grains

1 troy ounce (oz.t.) = 20 pennyweights, or 480 grains

1 troy pound (lb.t.) = 12 troy ounces, or 5,760 grains

APOTHECARIES' MEASURES

Apothecaries' measures are used to measure medicines. Apothecaries' measures are like troy weights, but they include some liquid measures as well as solid weights.

1 scruple = 20 grains

1 dram = 3 scruples, or 60 grains

1 apothecaries' ounce = 8 drams, or 480 grains

1 apothecaries' pound = 12 apothecaries' ounces, or 5,760 grains

1 fluid dram = 60 minims = 1 fluid ounce = 8 fluid drams

1 minim or drop = 1/60 fluid dram, or 1/480 fluid ounce

Metric Weights

In the 1790s, French scientists devised the **metric** system. The system covered measurement of length (see p. 67), area (see p. 76), volume (see p. 77), and weight. The basic unit of weight in the metric system is the **gram**.

METRIC AND U.S. CUSTOMARY WEIGHT EQUIVALENTS

Metric	Abbreviation	Metric Equivalent	U.S. Customary Equivalent
milligram	mg	.001 gram	.0154 grains
centigram	cg	10 milligrams	.154 grains
decigram	dg	10 centigrams	1.5432 grains
gram	g	1,000 milligrams	.0353 ounce
decagram	dag	10 grams	.353 ounce
hectogram	hg	100 grams	3.53 ounces
kilogram	kg	1,000 grams	2.204 pounds
metric ton	m.t.	1,000 kilograms	2,204 pounds (1.102 tons)

Why "Lb." for "Pound"?

The abbreviation **lb.** comes from the Latin **libra**, meaning "pound balance." When the English adopted the pound measure, they kept the Latin abbreviation.

3 Measuring Perimeter and Area

To measure flat spaces, like polygons (see p.101), we calculate **perimeter** and **area**. Perimeter is the distance around a polygon. **Area** is the size of a flat surface in square units.

Calculating Perimeter

Perimeter is calculated in different ways, depending upon the shape of the surface. The perimeter of a surface outlined by straight lines is calculated by adding together the lengths of its sides.

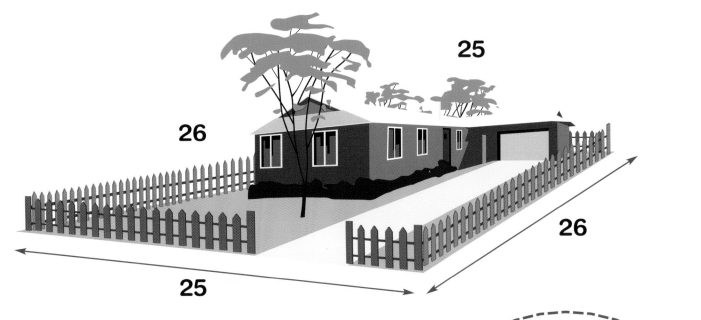

25

26

26

25

25 + 26 + 25 + 26 = perimeter of the fence

The perimeter of a circle (see p. 105) is called **circumference**. Mathematicians calculate circumference with a special equation:

circumference = πd or 2πr

The equations are read "**circumference equals pi times diameter**" or "**circumference equals two times pi times radius**." Diameter is the length of a line drawn across a circle through its center. Radius is half of the diameter, or a line drawn from the center of a circle to any point on the circle.

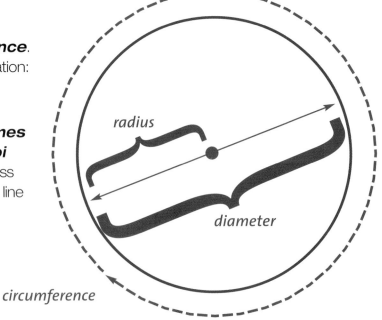

radius

diameter

circumference

Pi, or π, is the sixteenth letter of the Greek alphabet. In math, π has a special meaning: It stands for the ratio of a circle's diameter to its circumference; a number that is approximately equal to 3.14 or $^{22}/_7$.

π is used in many equations. For example:

circumference = pi × diameter, or πd

area of a circle = pi × radius squared, or πr^2

volume of a sphere = $\frac{4}{3}$ × pi × radius cubed, or $\frac{4\pi r^2}{3}$

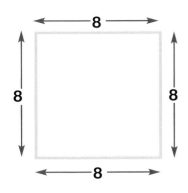

$8 + 8 + 8 + 8 = 4 \times 8 = 32$
4s (4 sides) =
perimeter of a square

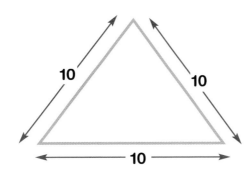

$10 + 10 + 10 = 30$
3s (3 sides) =
perimeter of an equilateral triangle

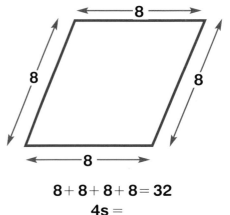

$8 + 8 + 8 + 8 = 32$
4s =
perimeter of a rhombus

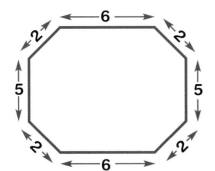

$5 + 2 + 6 + 2 + 5 + 2 + 6 + 2 = 30$
8s =
perimeter of a regular octagon

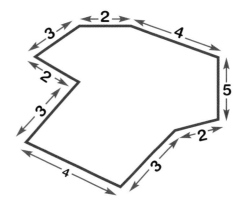

$4 + 3 + 2 + 3 + 2 + 4 + 5 + 2 + 3 = 28$
all sides =
perimeter of an irregular polygon

Calculating Area

Area, like perimeter, is calculated in different ways, depending on the shape of the surface. Area is expressed in squares: square inches, square meters, etc.

An area with a perimeter made up of straight lines (see Polygons, p. 101) is calculated in different ways for different shapes:

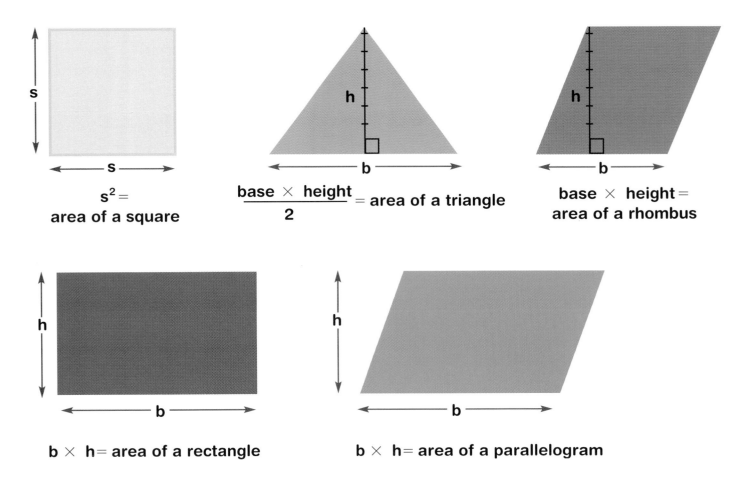

$$s^2 =$$
area of a square

$$\frac{base \times height}{2} = \textbf{area of a triangle}$$

$$base \times height =$$
area of a rhombus

$$b \times h = \textbf{area of a rectangle}$$

$$b \times h = \textbf{area of a parallelogram}$$

The area of a circle has a special calculation:

$$a = \pi r^2$$

The equation is read "**area equals pi times radius squared**."

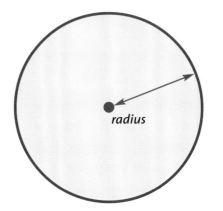

radius

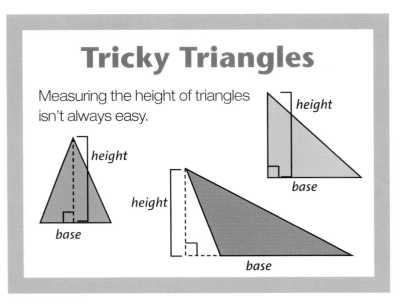

Tricky Triangles

Measuring the height of triangles isn't always easy.

height

base

height

base

height

base

Chapter 4 Measuring Volume

Volume is the amount of space contained in a three-dimensional shape. Area is a measurement of only **two** dimensions, usually length and width (see p. 76). Volume is a measurement of **three** dimensions, usually **length**, **width**, and **height**, and is measured in cubic units.

Calculating Volume

To find the volume of a **cube** or a **rectangular prism**, multiply length by width by height.

> Liquids and gases can only be measured by volume. They have their own U.S. Customary and Metric measures (see p. 79).

$$l \times w \times h = \text{volume of a rectangular prism}$$

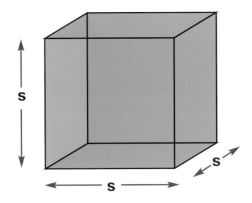

Since a cube has sides of equal length, multiply the length of one side by itself three times, s^3:

$$s^3 = \text{volume of a cube}$$

To find the volume of a **pyramid**, multiply the area of the base (B) or (s × s) by the height of the pyramid. Then divide the product by **3**.

$$\frac{B \times h}{3} = \text{ volume of a pyramid}$$

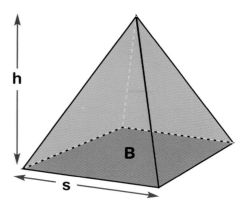

To find the volume of a **cylinder**, multiply the area of the base (B) or (πr^2) by the height of the cylinder.

$$\left. \begin{array}{c} B \times h \\ \pi r^2 \times h \end{array} \right\} = \text{ volume of a cylinder}$$

To find the volume of a **cone**, multiply the area of the base (B) or (πr^2) by the height of the cone. Then divide the product by **3**.

$$\left. \begin{array}{c} \dfrac{B \times h}{3} \\ \dfrac{\pi r^2 \times h}{3} \end{array} \right\} = \text{ volume of a cone}$$

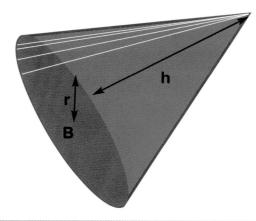

To calculate the volume of a **sphere**, multiply π by r^3. Then multiply the product by **4/3**.

$$\frac{4\pi r^3}{3} = \text{ volume of a sphere}$$

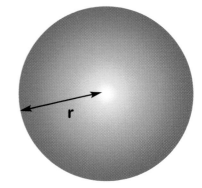

METRIC VOLUME MEASURES

10 milliliters (ml)	=	1 centiliter (cl)		
10 centiliter	=	1 deciliter (dl)	=	100 milliliters
10 deciliters	=	1 liter (l)	=	1,000 milliliters
1 liter(s)	=	10 deciliters (dl)	=	100 centiliters
10 liters	=	1 dekaliter (dal)		
10 dekaliters	=	1 hectoliter (hl)	=	100 liters
10 hectoliters	=	1 kiloliter (kl)	=	1,000 liters

U.S. CUSTOMARY LIQUID VOLUME MEASURES

Measure	Abbreviation	Equivalent
gill	gi.	4 ounces
cup	c.	8 ounces
pint	pt.	2 cups
quart	qt.	2 pints
gallon	gal.	4 quarts
barrel	bar.	31.5 gallons

U.S. CUSTOMARY CUBIC VOLUME MEASURES

1,728 cubic inches	=	1 cubic foot
27 cubic feet	=	1 cubic yard
16 cubic feet	=	1 cord foot
8 cord feet	=	1 cord

Measuring Temperature

The Fahrenheit Scale

About 300 years ago, German physicist Gabriel Daniel Fahrenheit (1686–1736) invented a scale for measuring heat. His scale is still used today on thermometers, oven dials, water heaters, and thermostats.

On Fahrenheit's scale, water freezes at 32°F and boils at 212°F. The 0°F mark was reached by mixing equal weights of snow (solid water) and salt. Of course, the "F" in the temperature readings stands for **Fahrenheit**!

The Centigrade Scale

In 1742, Swedish astronomer Anders Celsius (1701–1744) invented another scale for measuring heat. His scale is called the **centigrade** or **Celsius** scale. Celsius's scale is based on the freezing and boiling points of water. The freezing point of water is equal to 0°C. The boiling point is 100°C. While the Fahrenheit scale is used in the United States, the centigrade scale is used in most countries throughout the world. It is the scale preferred by scientists.

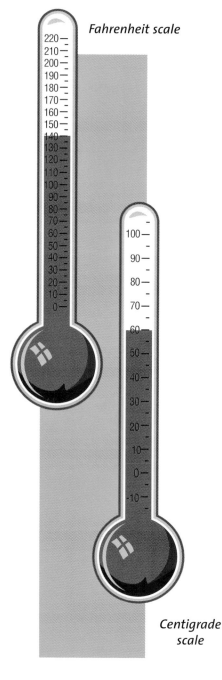

Fahrenheit scale

Centigrade scale

To convert from Fahrenheit to centigrade, subtract 32° from the Fahrenheit temperature and multiply the difference by 5. Then divide the product by 9.

$$\frac{5 \, (F \times 32)}{9}$$

To convert centigrade to Fahrenheit, multiply the centigrade temperature by 9, divide the product by 5, and add 32°:

$$\frac{(C \times 9)}{5} + 32$$

FAHRENHEIT/CENTIGRADE EQUIVALENTS

°F	°C	°C	°F
0	–17.8	–50	–58
10	–12.2	0	32
20	–6.67	10	50
32	0	20	68
40	4.44	30	86
50	10	40	104
100	37.78	50	122
212	100	100	212

Absolute Zero

William Thomson, Lord Kelvin (1824–1907), devised a scale based on *absolute zero*, the lowest possible temperature for any substance. The 0° mark on the Kelvin scale is equal to −459° on the Fahrenheit scale or −273° on the centigrade scale!

Brrrrrrrrrrrrrrrrrrrrrrrrrrrrr!

The lowest temperature on earth, −112°F or −80°C, was recorded in Antarctica. The lowest body temperature in a warm-blooded animal was recorded at a fraction above freezing in hibernating hamsters.

Hot Stuff!

Fahrenheit and centigrade scales are used to measure body temperature. A healthy body temperature is around 98.6° F or 37°C.

But where does body heat come from?

WHAT IS A CALORIE?

Body heat comes primarily from eating food. The heat is measured in calories and *kilocalories*, or 1,000 calories. A calorie is a metric measure. It stands for the amount of heat needed to raise the temperature of *1* gram of water *1* degree centigrade. By measuring the kilocalories in the foods we eat, we can tell how much heat we can generate, or how many kilocalories we can "burn" in daily activities (kilocalories are often called large calories).

CALORIES AND YOUR BODY WEIGHT

On days when you eat fewer calories than the number of calories you burn doing activities, you will burn calories stored in the fat and muscles in your body. On days when you eat more calories than you burn through activities, your body will store the excess calories in the form of fat. So, when you eat too little, your body burns up fat. You might then lose weight. When you eat too much, your body stores calories as fat. You might even gain weight.

apple	117 calories
hot dog	170 calories
slice of pizza	185 calories
banana	100 calories
chocolate (1 oz.)	155 calories
carrot	25 calories
spinach	23 calories

Note: Calories are approximate and vary according to serving size.

Measuring Time

A day, or twenty-four hours, is the time it takes earth to spin around once on its axis. (The axis is an imaginary pole that runs through the middle of the planet from the North Pole to the South Pole.) Seven days make up one week. Twenty-eight to thirty-one days make up one **month**. A month is the approximate time needed for the moon to revolve once around earth. The lunar month actually takes twenty-nine days, twelve hours, forty-four minutes, and three seconds.

Twelve months make up one **year**. A year is the time it takes the earth to revolve once around the sun, or 365 days, five hours, forty-eight minutes, and forty-six seconds.

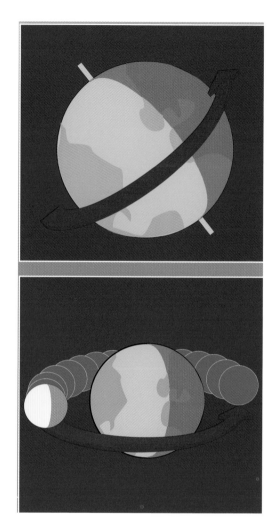

Ancient and Modern Calendars

Calendars are tools that help us group days into weeks, months, and years. The calendar used throughout the world today is called the **Gregorian** calendar. Several other calendars are also in use. Among them are Hebrew, Christian, Eastern Orthodox, Moslem, and Hindu calendars. These calendars start on different days, and divide the year according to different seasons and months. Most people today use one or two calendars—the Gregorian calendar and a religious calendar. The ancient Egyptians used three calendars at once! One was a calendar divided into 365 days. Another was a farmer's calendar based on the seasons. And the third was a religious calendar.

THE BABYLONIAN CALENDAR

The calendar used in ancient Babylon divided the year into 354 days. The days were grouped into twelve twenty-nine-day "months" or cycles of the moon. Eleven extra days were added at the end of each year to bring this calendar based on moon cycles in line with the 365-day cycle of the sun.

THE EGYPTIAN CALENDAR

The ancient Egyptians used a calendar that divided the year into twelve months of thirty days each. Five days were added at the end of each year to bring the calendar to 365 days.

THE CHINESE CALENDAR

The Chinese calendar divides the year into 365 days. It also groups years into cycles of twelve years each. Each year within the cycle is named for an animal.

RAT	OX	TIGER	HARE	DRAGON	SNAKE
1900	1901	1902	1903	1904	1905
1912	1913	1914	1915	1916	1917
1924	1925	1926	1927	1928	1929
1936	1937	1938	1939	1940	1941
1948	1949	1950	1951	1952	1953
1960	1961	1962	1963	1964	1965
1972	1973	1974	1975	1976	1977
1984	1985	1986	1987	1988	1989
1996	1997	1998	1999	2000	2001

HORSE	SHEEP	MONKEY	ROOSTER	DOG	BOAR
1906	1907	1908	1909	1910	1911
1918	1919	1920	1921	1922	1923
1930	1931	1932	1933	1934	1935
1942	1943	1944	1945	1946	1947
1954	1955	1956	1957	1958	1959
1966	1967	1968	1969	1970	1971
1978	1979	1980	1981	1982	1983
1990	1991	1992	1993	1994	1995
2001	2003	2004	2005	2006	2007

THE HEBREW CALENDAR

The Hebrew, or Jewish, calendar is a lunar calendar. It is based on months of a standard length, with months (called Adar II) added every third, sixth, eighth, eleventh, fourteenth, seventeenth, and nineteenth year over a 29-year period.

ניסן Nisan	תמוז Tammuz	תשרי Tishrei	טבת Tevet
אייר Iyar	אב Av	חשון Cheshvan	שבט Shevat
סיון Sivan	אלול Elul	כסלו Kislev	אדר Adar

CHRISTIAN CALENDARS

The calendar of the Christian Church is divided into seasons based on the life of Christ. More than 1,000 years ago, the Church split into eastern and western divisions. Although the seasons celebrated in the eastern and western churches are the same,

> **Advent**
>
> **Christmastide**
>
> **Lent**
>
> **Eastertide**
>
> **Pentecost**

the calendars are now different from each other, so the holidays are celebrated on different days.

THE HINDU CALENDAR

The Hindu calendar is based on lunar "days." There are thirty days in each month. So every Hindu day is $\frac{1}{30}$ of the moon's cycle. It is not the same as the solar day.

THE ISLAMIC CALENDAR

The Islamic calendar is a lunar calendar of twelve months of twenty-nine to thirty days each. There is no time added to bring the calendar in line with solar years. Holidays on the Islamic calendar "float" through the seasons as the years pass by.

If Your Birthday Is February 29, How Old Are You?

When Sosigenes created the Julian calendar, he divided the year into 365 days. But a solar year is really about 365¼ days long.

Sosigenes needed to make up for lost time. He decided to add a twenty-ninth day to February every fourth year. We call these long years **leap years**.

But what if you are born on February 29? Your birthday comes only once every four years. On your first "birthday," are you four years old?

Most leap-year babies celebrate their birthdays on February 28 or March 1 on non-leap years.

84

THE ROMAN CALENDAR

The ancient Romans began their year on March 1, the first day of the farming season. The calendar divided the year into ten lunar months and later into twelve lunar months. Extra days were added at the end of each year, but the calculation of how many days to add was done so badly, that by the time of Julius Caesar, the calendar no longer matched the seasons correctly. It was fixed in 46 B.C. (46 years before the Christian era) by the emperor Julius Caesar (see Julian calendar, below).

THE JULIAN CALENDAR

The astronomer Sosigenes was asked by Julius Caesar to create a calendar for the Roman Empire. The calendar was based on the solar year of 365 days. The year was divided into twelve months. Each month lasted thirty or thirty-one days, with the exception of February, which lasted either twenty-eight or twenty-nine days. The Julian calendar is the basis for the Gregorian calendar. The names used for the months in the Roman calendar were used in the Julian calendar. These names are also used today.

Roman	Gregorian	Roman	Gregorian
Januarius	January	Quintilis	July
Februarius	February	Sextilis	August
Martius	March	September	September
Aprilis	April	October	October
Maius	May	November	November
Junius	June	December	December

Days of the Week

The names we use for weekdays come from the Saxons of England. The Saxons named the days for the planets and their gods.

Sun's day . . . . Sunday		Thor's day . . . . . Thursday
Moon's day . . . . . Monday		Frigg's day . . . . Friday
Tiw's day . . . . Tuesday		Saturn's day . . . . Saturday
Woden's day . . Wednesday		

THE GREGORIAN CALENDAR

Sosigenes made a mistake in the Julian calendar, but nobody found the mistake for hundreds of years. He made every fourth year a leap year, but these leap years made the calendar too long to measure the cycle of the sun. By the 1500s, the Julian calendar was almost two weeks ahead of the actual solar year.

Pope Gregory VIII fixed the mistake in 1582. Leap years are now added to the calendar every four years, except for the years that begin new centuries, unless the number of the new century can be divided evenly by 400. For example, the century date 1900 was not a leap year

(1900 ÷ 400 = 4 ¾)

but the year 2000 was a leap year

(2000 ÷ 400 = 5).

Pope Gregory VIII's calendar is accurate to within sixteen seconds per year. That's the reason we still use it today.

JANUARY

SUNDAY	MONDAY	TUESDAY	WEDNESDAY	THURSDAY	FRIDAY	SATURDAY
				1	2	3
4	5	6	7	8	9	10
11	12	13	14	15	16	17
18	19	20	21	22	23	24
25	26	27	28	29	30	31

Ben Franklin and the Lost Days

News of the error in the Julian calendar traveled slowly. It was not until 1752 that the British colonists in North America changed from the Julian to the Gregorian calendar. By that time, the Julian calendar was eleven days off the solar year. To adjust to the new calendar, the colonists simply skipped the days between September 2 and September 14, 1752.

According to Ben Franklin, " . . . those who love their pillow [will] lie down in Peace on the second of this month and not perhaps awake until the morning of the fourteenth."

Clocks

We divide **days** into 24 **hours**, but hours are divided into 60 parts. Why?

The ancient Babylonians used a base 60 method for counting, unlike our base 10, or decimal system (see p. 16). A base 60 system was used to divide the globe into six groups of 60 minutes each, and to divide the hours into 60 equal parts.

Roman astronomers later adopted this system of dividing hours. They called each division a **par minuta** or "small part of an hour." From the Latin name comes our word **minute**. These early astronomers also divided minutes into 60 equal parts. They called each division **par seconda**, or **second**.

DAYLIGHT SAVING TIME

During World War I, clocks in the United States and England were set one hour ahead. By setting the clocks ahead in the summertime, the wartime work day had one more hour of daylight. The clocks were set back in autumn, when daylight hours were shorter anyway. Working in daylight meant saving energy because electric lights weren't needed to light up the factories.

Setting the clocks ahead also meant more hours of daylight for play and leisure activites. When the war ended, people still wanted to enjoy the extra hours of summer daylight. Daylight Saving Time was here to stay!

> **Daylight saving rule: spring forward, fall back.**

Not everybody in the United States uses Daylight Saving Time. People in Hawaii and parts of Indiana and Arizona don't reset their clocks. But most Americans set their clocks one hour ahead on the first Sunday in April and back one hour on the last Sunday of October.

Military Time

Standard Time	24-Hour Time	Military Time	Standard Time	24-Hour Time	Military Time
12:01 a.m.	00:00	0001 hours	12:00 (noon)	12:00	1200 hours
1:00 a.m.	01:00	0100 hours	1:00 p.m.	13:00	1300 hours
2:00 a.m.	02:00	0200 hours	2:00 p.m.	14:00	1400 hours
3:00 a.m.	03:00	0300 hours	3:00 p.m.	15:00	1500 hours
4:00 a.m.	04:00	0400 hours	4:00 p.m.	16:00	1600 hours
5:00 am.	05:00	0500 hours	5:00 p.m.	17:00	1700 hours
6:00 a.m.	06:00	0600 hours	6:00 p.m.	18:00	1800 hours
7:00 a.m.	07:00	0700 hours	7:00 p.m.	19:00	1900 hours
8:00 a.m.	08:00	0800 hours	8:00 p.m.	20:00	2000 hours
9:00 a.m.	09:00	0900 hours	9:00 p.m.	21:00	2100 hours
10:00 a.m.	10:00	1000 hours	10:00 p.m.	22:00	2200 hours
11:00 a.m.	11:00	1100 hours	11:00 p.m.	23:00	2300 hours
			12:00 (midnight)	24:00	2400 hours

Standard time can be confusing. For example, eight o'clock can mean eight in the morning or eight in the evening. To avoid confusion, scientists created a 24-hour clock. The hours are numbered **1** through **24**, beginning at midnight. This way of counting the hours in a day is called **military time**. People who use military time say the time in a special way. For example, 11:00 is not called "eleven o'clock," but "eleven hundred hours."

BEYOND STANDARD TIME

Standard time means the measurement of the day in two blocks of twelve hours each. The twelve hours from midnight to just before noon are **a.m.** hours. The twelve hours from noon until just before midnight are **p.m.** hours. The abbreviations "a.m." and "p.m." come from the Latin for **ante meridiem** and **post meridiem**, meaning **before** (ante) and **after** (post) midday or noon (**meridiem**).

SHADOW STICKS

Among the earliest timepieces were **shadow sticks**. The length and direction of the stick's shadow changes as the sun moves across the sky. The length and direction of a shadow give a rough idea of the time of day.

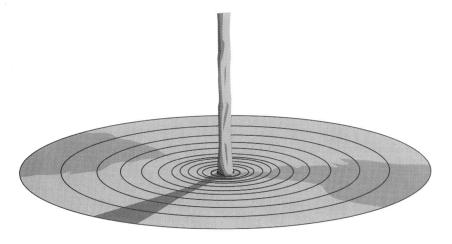

SUNDIALS

Like **shadow sticks**, **sundials** use shadows to show the time. Sundials, however, have a face with numbers that stand for the hours of sunlight. A stick, or gnomon, casts a shadow that falls on the face. The time is told by reading the number on the face where the shadow falls. But you can only tell time on a sunny day!

WATER CLOCKS

Water clocks are made by **calibrating**, or marking, the inside of a container that has a hole in its bottom. The container is filled with water and the water drips out slowly through the hole. Time is told by reading the water level in the container.

More than 3,000 years ago, the ancient Egyptians used water clocks called **clepsydras**. The Greeks and Romans used more complicated water clocks. Water was dripped from a reservoir, or a "holding tank," into a watertight cylinder. Time was told by reading a float in the cylinder.

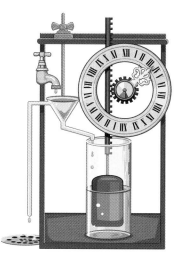

water clock

LAMPS AND CANDLE CLOCKS

The level of oil in a lamp shows how long the lamp has been burning. Reading the level of oil in a lit lamp or even the changes in length of a burning candle were other methods for telling time.

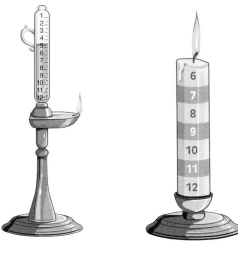

oil lamp   *candle clock*

SANDGLASSES

Sandglasses were invented hundreds of years ago. They are still used today as kitchen timers. Sandglasses have two chambers connected by a narrow neck. One chamber is filled with sand. When the sandglass is turned upside down or inverted, sand drips through the neck from the upper to the lower chamber. Time is measured when all the sand has passed to the lower chamber. In large sandglasses, or hourglasses, it takes sixty minutes for the sand to pass from the upper chamber to the lower chamber.

MECHANICAL CLOCKS

Mechanical clocks were invented more than 700 years ago. The first mechanical clocks didn't have hands and faces. Instead, they told the time with bells or chimes that rang out on the hours.

Italian astronomer and inventor Galileo Galilei (1564–1642) discovered that a swinging pendulum could keep time evenly. But it wasn't until 1657 that the first pendulum clock was invented. It was made by Dutch mathematician Christian Huygens (1629–1695).

Huygens's clock used swinging pendulums controlled by gears. The gears moved the hands of the clock across the clock face. Later, scientists discovered that a pendulum one meter long takes one second to complete a full arc backward and forward. Around 1670, the first clocks with pendulums one meter long were built.

Huygens's clock

QUARTZ

Today many clocks and watches use the battery-powered vibrations of a quartz crystal to keep time. The natural vibration of a quartz crystal is 100,000 times per second. Modern clocks and watches show the time in digital as well as analog displays.

Digital

Analog

Atomic hydrogen masers, or "atomic clocks," are the most accurate clocks. They are accurate to within one second in 1.7 million years. Hydrogen atoms make atomic clocks work. A hydrogen atom vibrates 9.2 billion times in one second.

Seconds, Please!

Seconds really add up. Have you ever wondered how many seconds there are in:

One Minute	= 60 seconds	Five Years	= 157,784,630 seconds
One Hour	= 3,600 seconds	Ten Years	= 315,569,260 seconds
One Day	= 86,400 seconds	Fifty Years	= 1,577,846,300 seconds
One Week	= 604,800 seconds	One Hundred	
One Year	= 31,556,926 seconds	Years	= 3,155,692,600 seconds

Greenwich Mean Time

The sun reaches its highest point in the sky at different times in different places around the world. That's why the earth is divided into twenty-four time zones, one zone for each hour of the day. These time zones loosely follow lines of longitude.

The time zones begin at the **prime meridian** in Greenwich, England, and meet at the **International Date Line**. If you travel east over the International Date Line, you start the day over again. If you travel west over the line, you jump ahead to the next day.

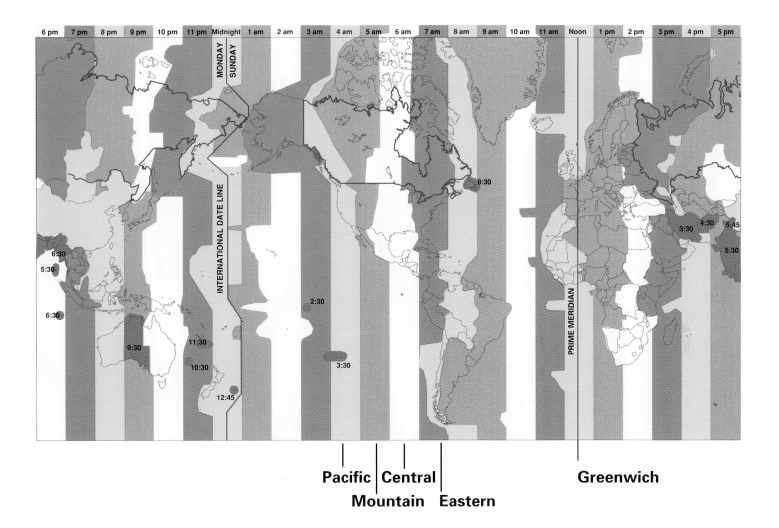

TABLE OF GREENWICH MEAN AND U.S. STANDARD TIME EQUIVALENTS

Greenwich	Eastern Time	Central Time	Mountain Time	Pacific Time
MIDNIGHT	7 p.m. (yesterday)	6 p.m. (yesterday)	5 p.m. (yesterday)	4 p.m. (yesterday)
1 a.m.	8 p.m. (yesterday)	7 p.m. (yesterday)	6 p.m. (yesterday)	5 p.m. (yesterday)
2 a.m.	9 p.m. (yesterday)	8 p.m. (yesterday)	7 p.m. (yesterday)	6 p.m. (yesterday)
3 a.m.	10 p.m. (yesterday)	9 p.m. (yesterday)	8 p.m. (yesterday)	7 p.m. (yesterday)
4 a.m.	11 p.m. (yesterday)	10 p.m. (yesterday)	9 p.m. (yesterday)	8 p.m. (yesterday)
5 a.m.	**MIDNIGHT**	11 p.m. (yesterday)	10 p.m. (yesterday)	9 p.m. (yesterday)
6 a.m.	1 a.m.	**MIDNIGHT**	11 p.m. (yesterday)	10 p.m (yesterday)
7 a.m.	2 a.m.	1 a.m.	**MIDNIGHT**	11 p.m. (yesterday)
8 a.m.	3 a.m.	2 a.m.	1 a.m.	**MIDNIGHT**
9 a.m.	4 a.m.	3 a.m.	2 a.m.	1 a.m.
10 a.m.	5 a.m.	4 a.m.	3 a.m.	2 a.m.
11 a.m.	6 a.m.	5 a.m.	4 a.m.	3 a.m.
NOON	7 a.m.	6 a.m.	5 a.m.	4 a.m.
1 p.m.	8 a.m.	7 a.m.	6 a.m.	5 a.m
2 p.m.	9 a.m.	8 a.m	7 a.m.	6 a.m.
3 p.m.	10 a.m.	9 a.m.	8 a.m.	7 a.m.
4 p.m.	11 a.m.	10 a.m.	9 a.m.	8 .am.
5 p.m.	**NOON**	11 a.m.	10 a.m.	9 a.m.
6 p.m.	1 p.m.	**NOON**	11 a.m.	10 a.m.
7 p.m.	2 p.m.	1 p.m.	**NOON**	11 a.m.
8 p.m.	3 p.m.	2 p.m.	1 p.m.	**NOON**
9 p.m.	4 p.m.	3 p.m.	2 p.m.	1 p.m.
10 p.m.	5 p.m.	4 p.m.	3 p.m.	2 p.m.
11 p.m.	6 p.m.	5 p.m.	4 p.m.	3 p.m.

Geometry

Chapter 1 Geometric Shapes

Geometry is the branch of mathematics that explains how **points**, **lines**, **planes**, and **shapes** are related.

Points

Points have no size or dimensions, that is, no width, length, or height. They are an **idea** and cannot be seen. But, points are used to tell the position of lines and objects. Points are usually named with capital letters:

A, **B**, **C**, **D** and so on.

Points can describe where things begin or end.

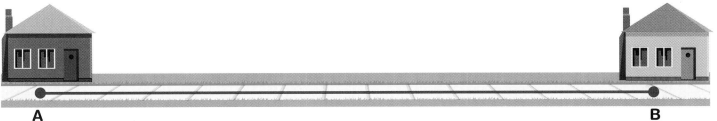

A   B

Points can be used to measure distance.

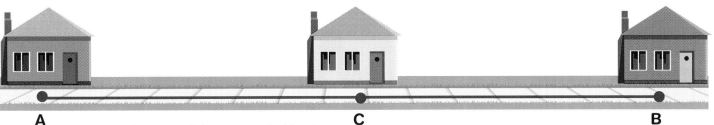

A   C   B

Points define the perimeter of shapes and objects.

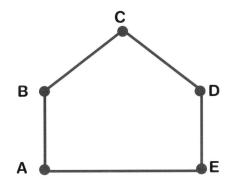

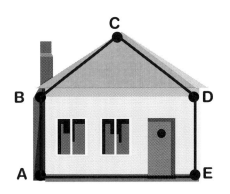

Lines

Lines extend in opposite directions and go on without ending. Like points, lines have no volume, but they have infinite length. Lines are named by points with a line symbol written above them.

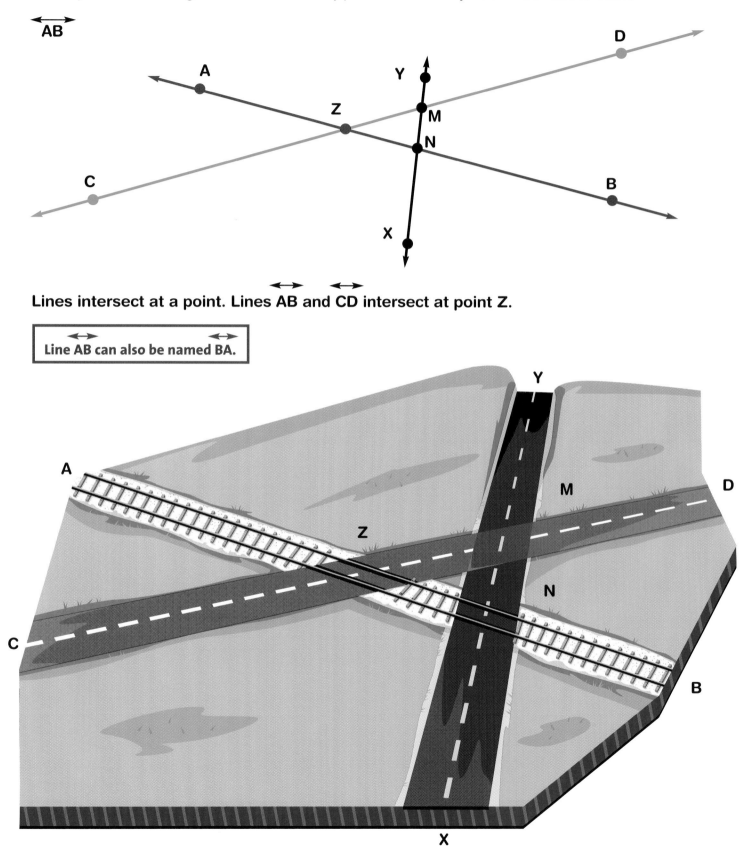

Lines intersect at a point. Lines $\overleftrightarrow{AB}$ and $\overleftrightarrow{CD}$ intersect at point Z.

Line $\overleftrightarrow{AB}$ can also be named $\overleftrightarrow{BA}$.

Line Segments

Line segments are parts of lines defined by two endpoints along the line. They have *length*.

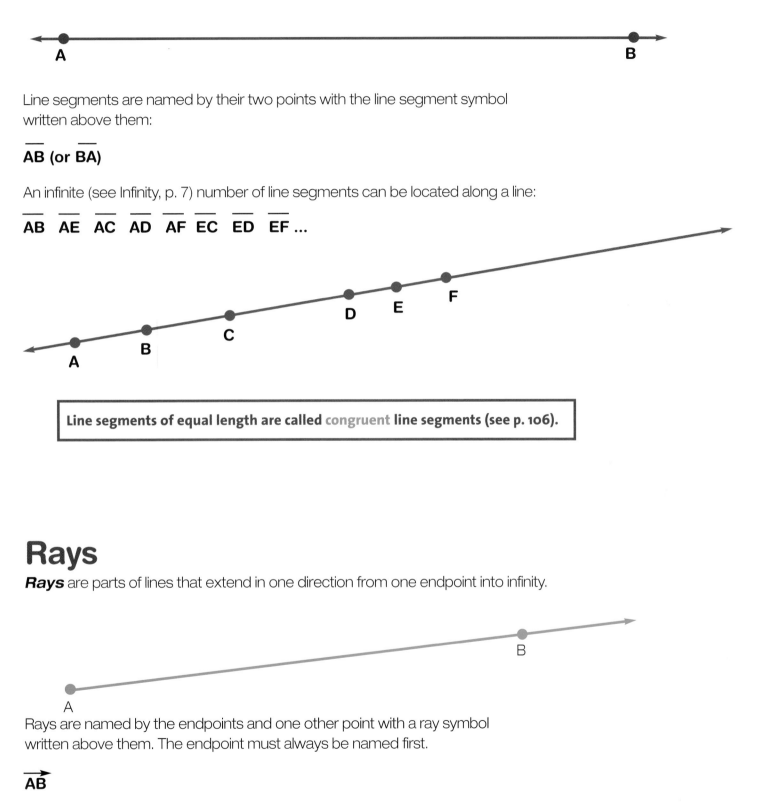

Line segments are named by their two points with the line segment symbol written above them:

$\overline{AB}$ (or $\overline{BA}$)

An infinite (see Infinity, p. 7) number of line segments can be located along a line:

$\overline{AB}$ $\overline{AE}$ $\overline{AC}$ $\overline{AD}$ $\overline{AF}$ $\overline{EC}$ $\overline{ED}$ $\overline{EF}$ ...

Line segments of equal length are called congruent line segments (see p. 106).

Rays

Rays are parts of lines that extend in one direction from one endpoint into infinity.

Rays are named by the endpoints and one other point with a ray symbol written above them. The endpoint must always be named first.

$\overrightarrow{AB}$

Parallel Lines

Parallel lines lie within the same plane and are always the same distance apart. Parallel lines continue to infinity without intersecting or touching at any point.

The symbol for parallel lines is // and is read "is parallel to."

AB // CD

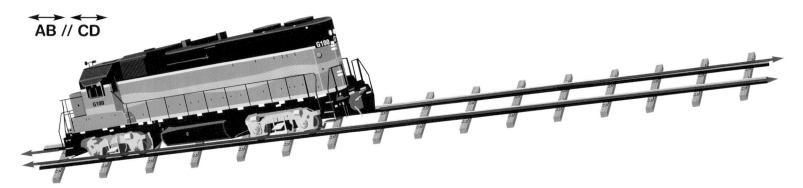

Intersecting Lines

Intersecting lines are lines in the same plane that meet and pass through one another at one point.

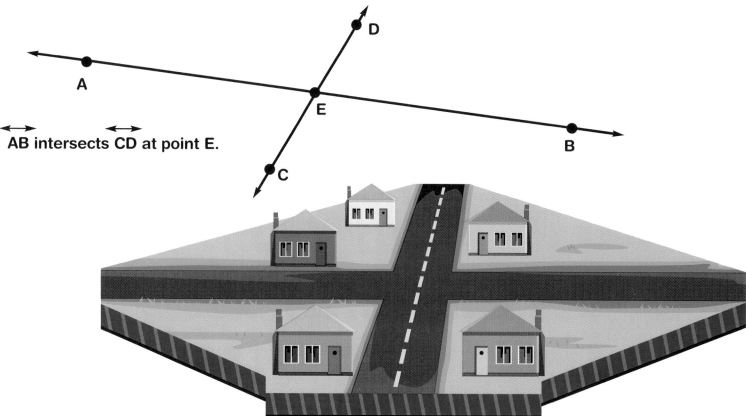

AB intersects CD at point E.

Perpendicular Lines

Perpendicular lines are intersecting lines that form right angles.

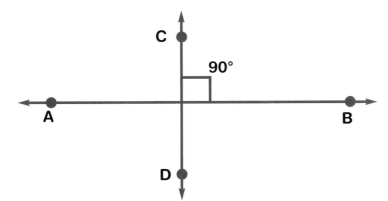

The symbol for perpendicular lines is ⊥ and is read "is perpendicular to."

 AB ⊥ CD

Planes

Planes are an infinite set of points that make up a flat surface. Planes extend in all directions to infinity but have no thickness.

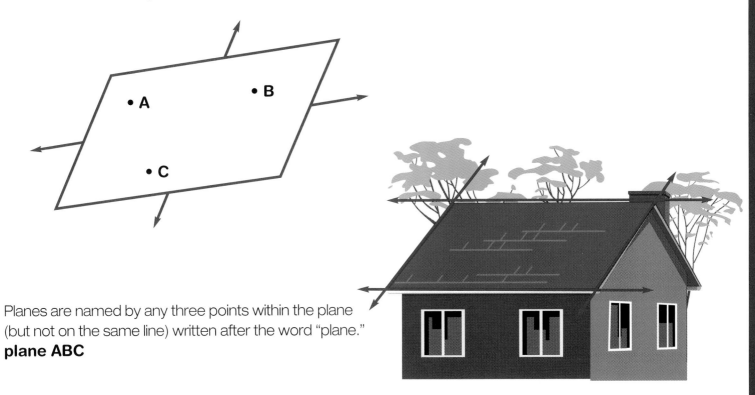

Planes are named by any three points within the plane (but not on the same line) written after the word "plane."
plane ABC

Angles

Angles are formed by two rays with a common endpoint called a *vertex*.

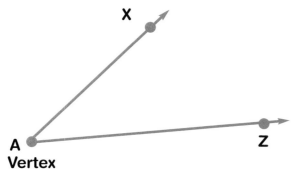

X

A
Vertex

Z

Angles are named by writing the names of three points on the set of lines after the angle symbol (∠), or by naming only the middle point after the angle symbol. The middle point always names the vertex.

∠ **XAZ**   or   ∠**ZAX**   or   ∠**A**

Angles come in different shapes and sizes. Some are narrow, some are wide. But all angles can be measured as part of a circle. To make calculations easy, scientists have developed the protractor, a kind of ruler for angles.

Angles are measured in degrees from 0° to 180°.

How to Use a Protractor

A *protractor* is an instrument used to measure angles. *Angles* are measured in *degrees* (°).
   To use a protractor to measure an angle, place the locator point on the *vertex* of the angle you wish to measure. Next, align one leg of the angle with the bottom leg of the protractor (at 0°). Then follow the other leg of the angle to measure its distance from 0°. In this illustration, the angle measures 110°.

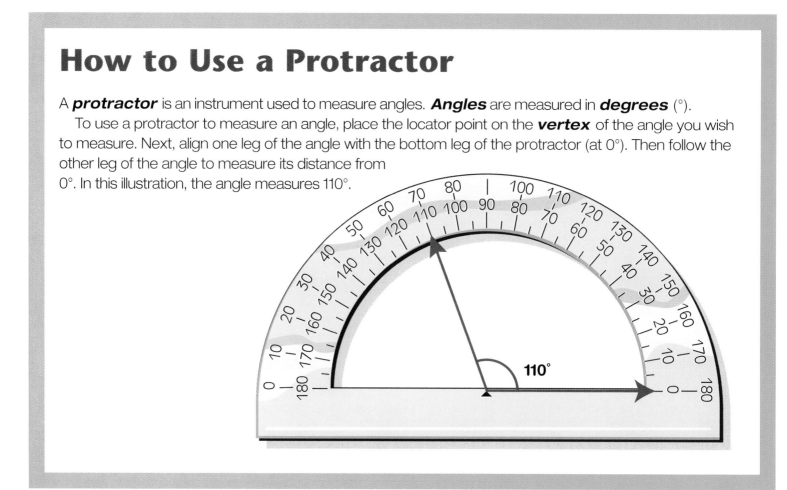

ACUTE ANGLES

Acute angles are angles that measure less than 90°.

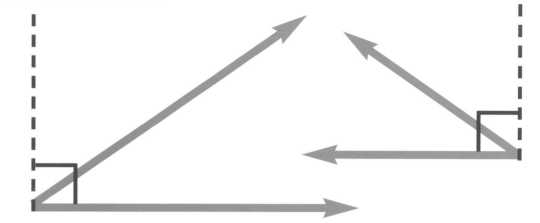

OBTUSE ANGLES

Obtuse angles are angles that measure more than 90° and less than 180°.

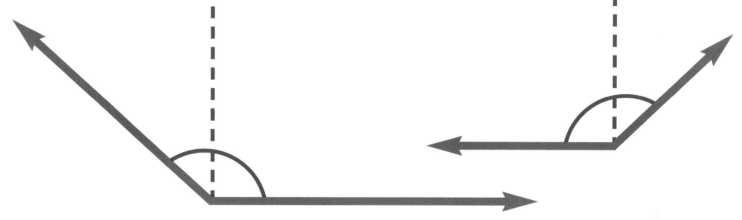

RIGHT ANGLES

Right angles are angles that measure exactly 90°.

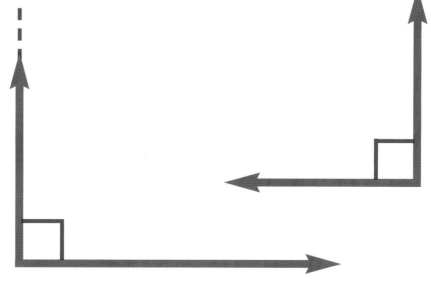

REFLEX ANGLES

Reflex angles are angles that measure more than 180°, but less than 360°.

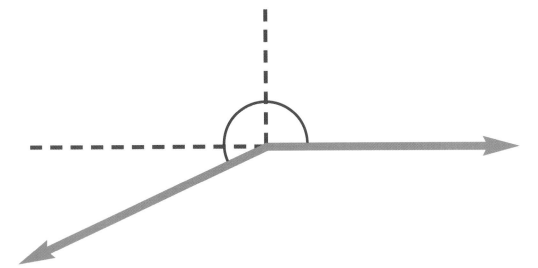

COMPLEMENTARY ANGLES

Complementary angles are angles that, when joined together, form a right angle (90°).

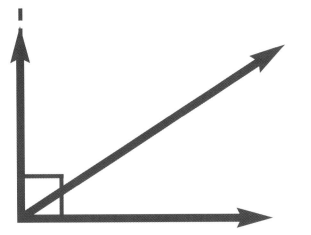

SUPPLEMENTARY ANGLES

Supplementary angles are angles that, when joined together, form a straight line (180°).

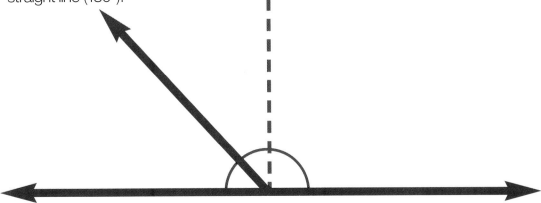

Polygons

Polygons are two-dimensional, or flat, shapes, formed from three or more line segments that lie within one plane. The line segments form angles that meet at points called *vertices*. Polygons come in many shapes and sizes, including:

concave polygons

convex polygons

> Polygons are irregular or regular. Irregular polygons are made up of unequal sides or unequal angles. Regular polygons have sides of equal length and angles of equal size.

Squares and equilateral triangles are examples of regular polygons.

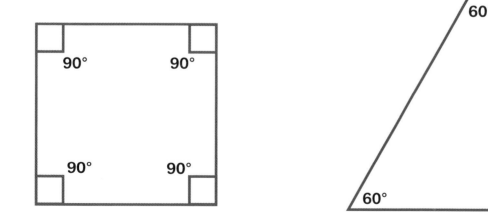

> The interior angles of all quadrilaterals always add up to 360°.
> The interior angles of all triangles always add up to 180°.

Triangles

Triangles are polygons that have three sides and three vertices.

Right triangles are formed when two of three line segments meet in 90-degree angles. In a right triangle, the longest side has a special name: the **hypotenuse**.

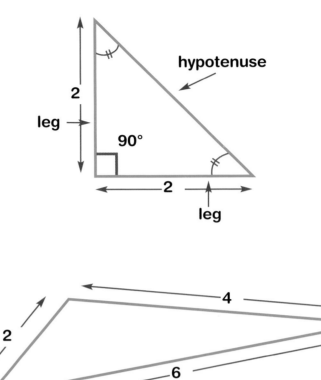

Isosceles triangles have only two sides of equal length.

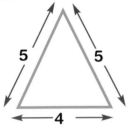

Scalene triangles have no sides of equal length.

Equilateral triangles have three sides of equal length.

Pythagoras's Great Idea

Pythagoras (ca.582–ca.497 B.C.) was a Greek philosopher and mathematician. His ideas influenced great thinkers throughout the ages, and he is well known to math students. His **Pythagorean theorem** is a simple rule about the proportion of the sides of right triangles: **The square of the hypotenuse of a right triangle is equal to the sum of the squares of the other two sides.**

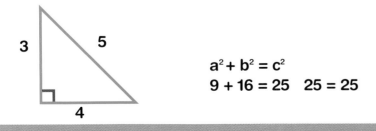

$$a^2 + b^2 = c^2$$
$$9 + 16 = 25 \quad 25 = 25$$

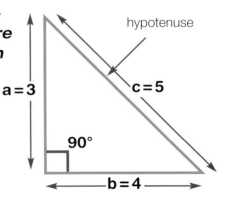

Quadrilaterals

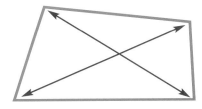

Quadrilaterals are polygons that have four sides and four vertices.

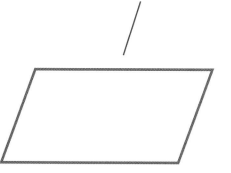

Parallelograms are quadrilaterals that have parallel line segments in both pairs of opposite sides.

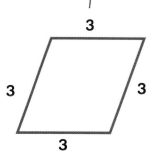

Trapezoids are quadrilaterals that have only one pair of parallel sides.

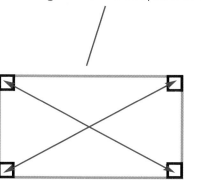

Rectangles are parallelograms formed by line segments that meet at right angles. A rectangle always has four right angles.

Rhombuses are parallelograms that have sides of equal length.

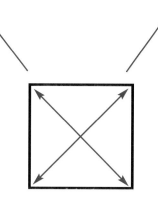

Squares are rectangles that, like rhombuses, have sides of equal length.

Other Common Polygons

PENTAGONS

Pentagons are polygons that have five sides and five vertices.

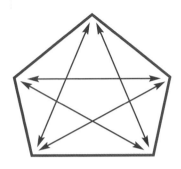

HEXAGONS

Hexagons are polygons that have six sides and six vertices.

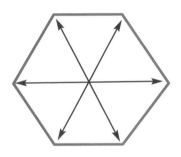

OCTAGONS

Octagons are polygons that have eight sides and eight vertices.

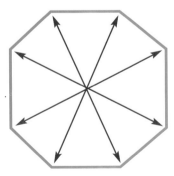

POLYGONS

Name	Number of sides	Sum (in degrees) of interior angles
triangle	3	180°
quadrilateral	4	360°
square	4 equal and perpendicular	360° 360°
rectangle	4 perpendicular	360°
rhombus	4 equal	360°
parallelogram	4 opposite parallel	360°
pentagon	5	900°
hexagon	6	1080°
heptagon	7	1260°
octagon	8	1440°
nonagon	9	1620°
decagon	10	1800°
ondecagon or hendecagon	11	1980°
dodecagon	12	2160°
icosagon	20	3600°

Circles

A **circle** is a set of points within a plane where all points on the circle's perimeter are at the same distance from a common point inside the circle, called the **center**.

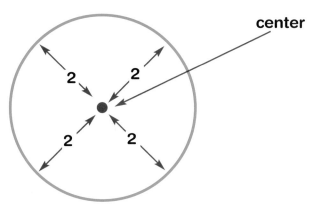

center

The distance from the center of the circle to any point on the circle is called the **radius**.

r = radius

A line segment drawn through the center of the circle to points on either side of the circle is called the **diameter**. The circle is bisected or cut into two equal parts along the diameter line. The diameter is equal to two times the **radius**.

2r = diameter

The distance around the circle is called the **circumference** (see p. 74).

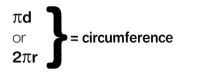

$$\left.\begin{matrix} \pi d \\ \text{or} \\ 2\pi r \end{matrix}\right\} = \text{circumference}$$

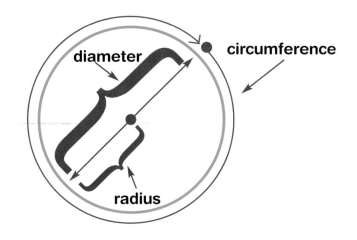

diameter

circumference

radius

Arcs, Chords, and Semicircles

Radius, diameter, and circumference are not the only terms used to describe the parts of a circle. Other terms include **arc**, **chord**, and **semicircle**.

An **arc** is a curved line drawn between two points along the **circumference** of a circle.

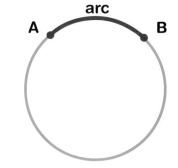

arc

A   B

A **chord** is a line drawn between two points on a circle.

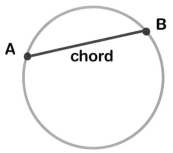

B

A   chord

A **semicircle** is an arc that is defined by diametric points along the circle. This arc is as large as half (semi) the circle.

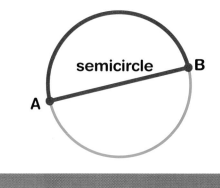

semicircle   B

A

Symmetry, Congruence, and Similarity

Symmetry surrounds us. It is found in art and architecture, music, plants, insects, animals—and humans.

Symmetry is the exact matching of shapes or figures on opposite sides of dividing lines or around a central point. The dividing line is called the **axis of symmetry** or **line of symmetry**. Certain shapes, particularly polygons and circles, have many lines of symmetry.

horizontal line of symmetry

vertical line of symmetry

Congruence refers to two shapes of exactly the same size and shape.

> The symbol for congruence is ≅ and is read "is congruent to."

A   **B**   **peanut A ≅ peanut B**

The symmetrical shapes formed by drawing a line of symmetry are congruent.

vertical line of symmetry makes congruent shapes

Similarity means objects have the same shape but they are not necessarily identical in size.

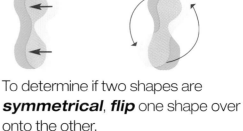

Congruent shapes are always similar.

The Elements of Geometry

Euclid (lived ca. 300 B.C.), a Greek mathematician who lived in Alexandria, Egypt, wrote one of the most famous textbooks of all time, **The Elements of Geometry**. Many people believe that Euclid's book has been read by more people than any other book except the Bible. Even our modern books on geometry are based on Euclid's 2,000-year-old teachings.

Slides, Rotations, and Flips

To determine if two shapes are **congruent**, **slide** one shape over the other, or **rotate** one shape over the other.

To determine if two shapes are **symmetrical**, **flip** one shape over onto the other.

Chapter 3 Objects in Three Dimensions

Polygons and circles are flat, or two-dimensional. They have only length and width. But **cubes**, **prisms**, **pyramids**, and **spheres** are solid. They have a third dimension known as height or, sometimes, depth. These solids are also called **space figures**.

Cubes, prisms, pyramids, and other solids have sides called **faces**. These faces are flat surfaces that are in the shapes of polygons. Faces meet at **edges**. The edges are line segments, which meet in vertexes. The vertexes are points (see p. 93).

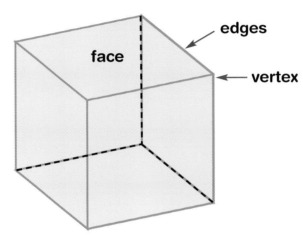

CUBES

Cubes have six faces. Each face is a square.

PRISMS

Prisms have two parallel, congruent, polygon-shaped *bases*. The sides of prisms are all parallelograms. Prisms can have an infinite variety of shapes because of the endless number of polygon shapes that can be used as bases. Each face that is not a base is called a *lateral face*.

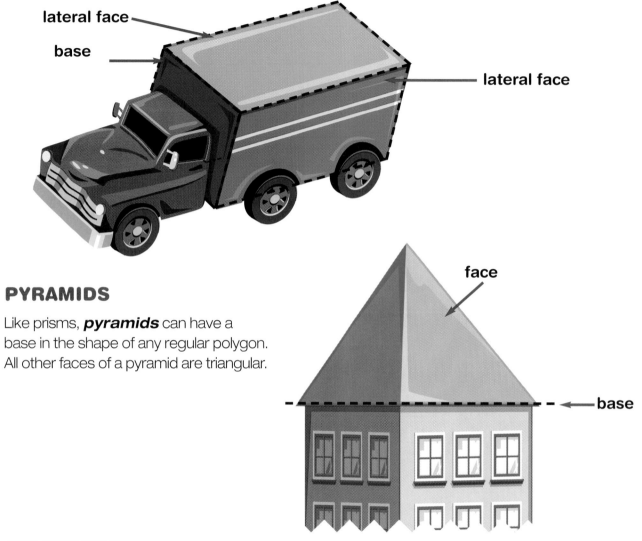

lateral face

base

lateral face

PYRAMIDS

Like prisms, *pyramids* can have a base in the shape of any regular polygon. All other faces of a pyramid are triangular.

face

base

CYLINDERS

Cylinders are solids with circles for bases and no vertexes.

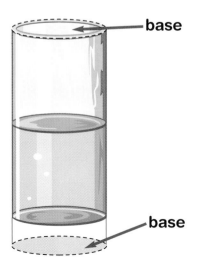

base

base

CONES

Cones have one flat, circular base and rise to a point. They have one base and one vertex.

vertex

base

SPHERES

Spheres have no flat faces and no vertexes. A sphere has an outline of a circle when viewed from any angle.

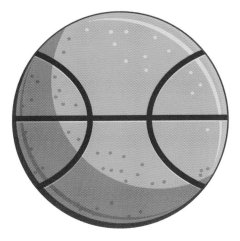

Fewer Facets

You can draw regular polygons (polygons with equal sides and angles) with any number of sides. However, you can't form an infinite number of regular solids (solids with equal sides and angles). In fact, you can form only five: **tetrahedron**, **cube**, **octahedron**, **dodecahedron**, and **icosahedron**.

Plane figure	Number of faces	Number of edges	Number of vertexes
cubes	6	12	8
prisms	6	12	8
pyramids	5	8	5
cylinders	3	2	0
cones	2	1	1
spheres	1	0	0

Chapter 1 # U.S. Currency

Mint Condition

dollar

quarter

dime

nickel

penny

Why Dollars and Cents?

British currency is made up of pounds and pence. Many other European countries use Euros and cents. Why do we use dollars and cents?

The word **dollar** comes from the German word for a large silver coin, the **Thaler**. In 1781, **cent** was suggested as a name for the smallest division of the dollar. Thomas Jefferson, third president of the United States and an amateur scientist, thought that the dollar should be divided into 100 parts. The word **cent** comes from the Latin **centum**, which means "one hundred."

There is a smaller value of U.S. money than the cent, although there is no coin for it. The value is called the **mill**. It is worth $\frac{1}{10}$ of a cent, or $.001.

What's Money? What's Currency?

Currency is the set of coins and bills issued by a government to be used as money. Not all money is currency. Before coins and bills became currency, humans used a variety of items as money. Stone disks, fur pelts, beads, and feathers have all served the purpose. And when coins were created, they were valued against the old items commonly traded as money. In ancient Greece, for example, the silver coin called the **drachma** was equal to a handful of iron nails. Since a handful of iron nails was the price for an ox, one **drachma** could buy one ox.

Place Value and American Money

American money is created in decimal-based currency. That means we can add, subtract, divide, and multiply money the same way we do any decimal numbers (see p. 48).

The basic unit of U.S. currency is the dollar. The dollar has the value of one on a place value chart. The decimal point separates dollars from cents, which are counted as tenths and hundredths in a place value chart.

$1.11	ones = dollars	.	tenths = dimes	hundredths = pennies
one cent		.	0	1
ten cents		.	1	0
one dollar	1	.	0	0

$4.63	ones = dollars	.	tenths = dimes	hundredths = pennies
three cents		.	0	3
sixty cents		.	6	0
four dollars	4	.	0	0

When you write down amounts of money using the dollar sign, **$**, you write the amounts the same way as you write decimal numbers—in decimal notation. There is a separate cents sign, **¢**. The cents sign does not use decimal notation. So if you have to add cents to dollars, you have to change cents to dollar notation. To add 8¢ to $1.03, convert the 8¢ notation to its decimal form, $.08. Then add the decimal fractions.

8¢ = $ .08
36¢ = $ .36

8¢ = $ .08
     + $1.03
       $1.11

CENTS IN DOLLAR NOTATION

¢	to	$
1		.01
2		.02
3		.03
4		.04
5		.05
10		.10
25		.25
100		1.00

Money Talks

break the bank	spend more than you have
broke	out of money
bucks	slang for "dollar bills"
budget	a plan for spending money over a period of time
cash	money in coins and bills
C-note	slang for "hundred-dollar bill"
dough	slang for "money"
(a) grand	slang for "thousand dollars"
greenbacks	U.S. paper money
moolah	slang for "money"
sawbuck	slang for "ten-dollar bill"
two bits	slang for "25¢"
K	one thousand dollars

Other Currency Systems

Money in Other Countries

Country	Name	Foreign currency in dollars (changes daily)
Argentina	Peso	.30
Belgium	Euro	1.07
Britain	Pound	1.50
China	Yuan	.12
Denmark	Krone	.15
France	Euro	1.07
Germany	Euro	1.07
India	Rupee	.03
Ireland	Euro	1.07
Israel	New Shekel	.21
Italy	Euro	1.07
Japan	Yen	.008
Mexico	Peso	.09
The Netherlands	Euro	1.07
Saudi Arabia	Riyal	.26
Thailand	Baht	.03

Using this chart, to change a U.S. dollar to British pounds, you divide.

$1 ÷ 1.5 = £.66 British pounds sterling.

To change a British pound to U.S. dollars, you multiply.

£1 x 1.5 = $1.50 U.S. dollars.

Graphs

Plotting Information

A **graph** is a kind of drawing or diagram that shows **data**, or information, usually in numbers. In order to make a graph, you must first have data.

Making a Simple Coordinate Graph

Many graphs show information on a **grid**. The grid is made up of lines that intersect to create a screen pattern. The bottom line of the grid is called the **horizontal axis** and the vertical line on the left or right is called the **vertical axis**.

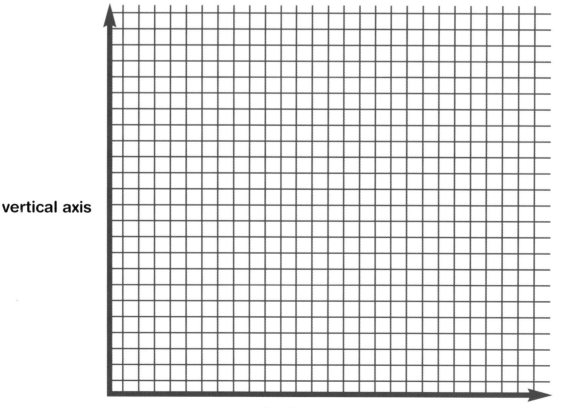

vertical axis

horizontal axis

> The horizontal axis is called the "*x*" axis, and the vertical axis is called the "*y*" axis.

Plotting and Locating Information on a Coordinate Graph

To plot or locate points on a coordinate graph, first locate the point according to its distance from **O** on the horizontal axis. Then move vertically the appropriate number of units to the next point.

A point on the graph is located by using an ordered pair. An ordered pair lists the horizontal and then the vertical location of the point. Ordered pairs are always written inside parentheses **( )**. The ordered pair describing the point J at right is (4, 3).

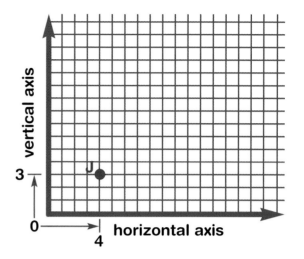

COORDINATE GRAPHS SHOWING POSITIVE AND NEGATIVE NUMBERS

Coordinate graphs can be drawn to show negative as well as positive coordinates.

Points on the graph are located the same way as on the simple coordinate graph, although the extended graph (in four quadrants) allows you to plot negative as well as positive coordinates. For example, the ordered pair describing the point A is (2, −3), and the ordered pair describing the point B is (−2, 3).

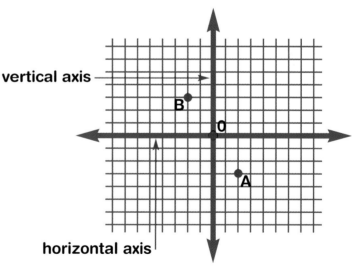

> **Points located on the same graph are called coordinate points or coordinates.**

Four Kinds of Graphs

Bar Graphs

Bar graphs are used to compare data. They can be **simple** or **complex**.
A simple bar graph can be made complex by adding data.

The Student Council at Jefferson Elementary held an ice cream-eating contest at the school fair.

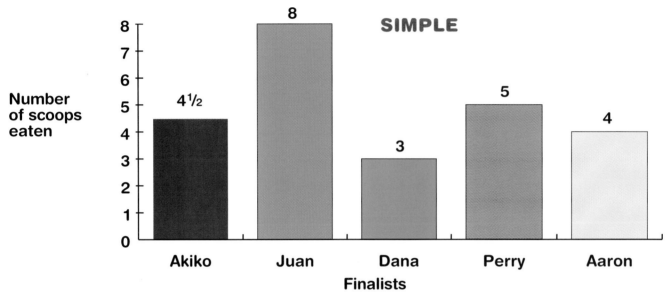

SIMPLE

Number of scoops eaten

Akiko 4½, Juan 8, Dana 3, Perry 5, Aaron 4

Finalists

To raise money for the Student Council, student teams sold tickets to the fair.

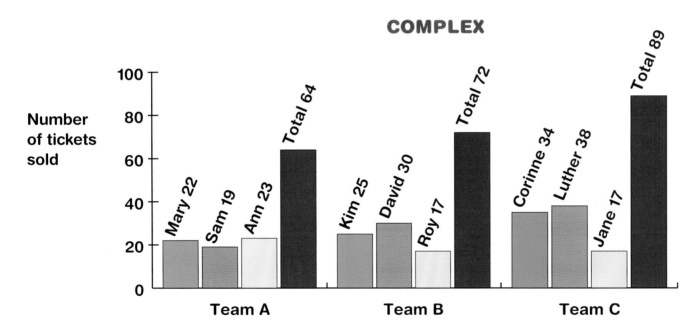

COMPLEX

Number of tickets sold

Team A: Mary 22, Sam 19, Ann 23, Total 64
Team B: Kim 25, David 30, Roy 17, Total 72
Team C: Corinne 34, Luther 38, Jane 17, Total 89

Pictographs

Pictographs are graphs that use pictures called **icons** to display data. Pictographs are used to show data in a small space. Pictographs, like bar graphs, compare data. Because pictographs use icons, however, they also include keys, or definitions of the icons.

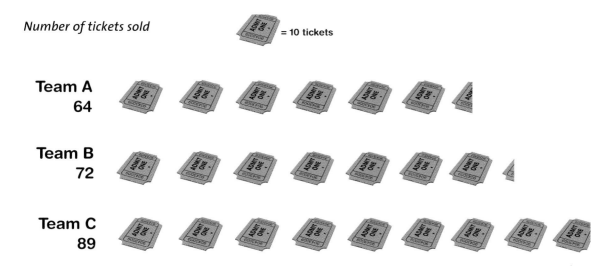

Number of tickets sold

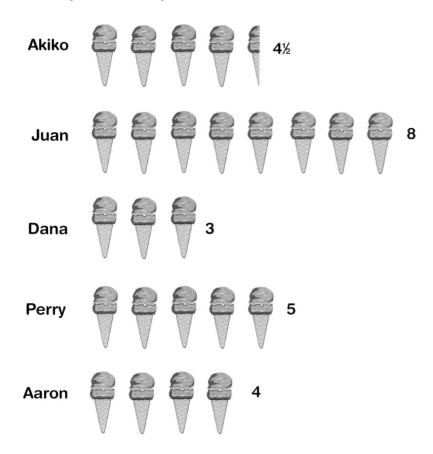

Number of ice cream scoops eaten

Line Graphs

Line graphs, unlike bar graphs and pictographs, show gradual changes in data.

The Student Council sold tickets to the school fair over a period of three weeks.

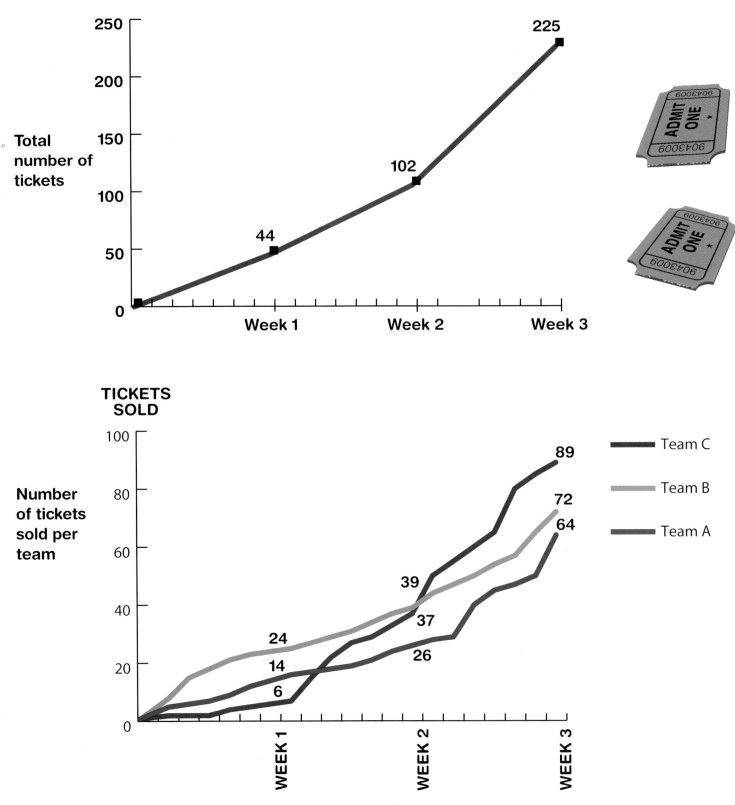

Circle Graphs

Circle graphs are also known as "pie" graphs, or pie charts. Circle graphs consist of a circle divided into parts. The different parts show the different proportions, or amounts, sizes, or numbers, of various data. To make circle graphs, raw data are compared by their relative proportions. Usually this is done by calculating percentages from the data and then plotting the percentages proportionally within a circle. That means each portion of a circle graph, when added together, will add up to 100%.

Number of ice cream scoops eaten in the contest

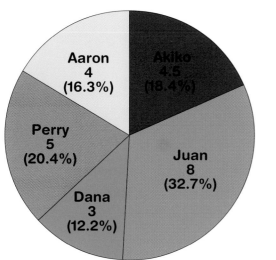

Raw data	Percentages
Aaron 4	(16.3%)
Akiko 4.5	(18.4%)
Juan 8	(32.7%)
Dana 3	(12.2%)
Perry 5	(20.4%)

Total number of scoops = 24.5 (100%)

Team ticket sales for the school fair, by team

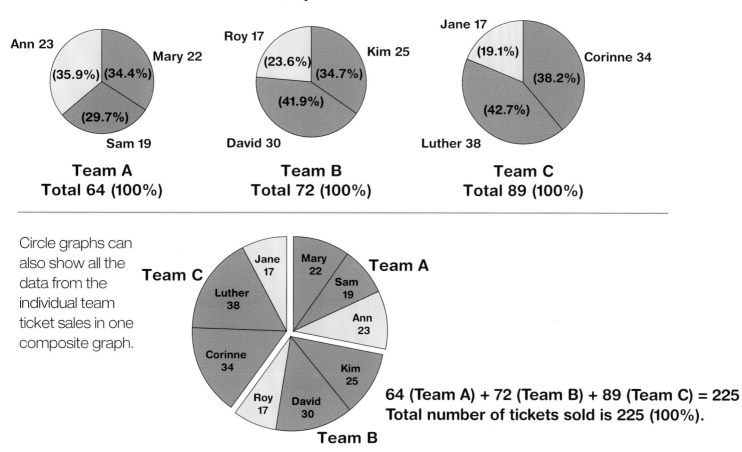

Circle graphs can also show all the data from the individual team ticket sales in one composite graph.

64 (Team A) + 72 (Team B) + 89 (Team C) = 225
Total number of tickets sold is 225 (100%).

Statistics and Probability

What Is Statistics?

Statistics is a branch of mathematics in which groups of numbers are compared. Statistics includes collecting, organizing, and interpreting data. Your attendance record at school provides your teachers with statistics on your participation in the classroom. Senators' voting attendance records on Capitol Hill are statistics that help us decide if they're doing a good job. Statistics are also used to compare athletes' achievements.

	Minutes	Free Throws	Fouls	Points
Anita	25	6	3	12
Jane	14	4	3	8
Caitlin	22	7	4	16
Josie	19	5	2	14
Tanisha	30	6	5	21
			Total	71

Statistics are often compared in graphs (see Graphs, pp. 114–119).

Minutes/points

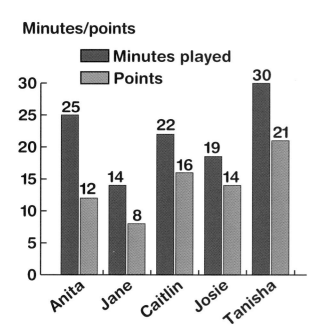

Points

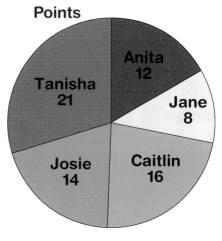

Total: 71

Free throws

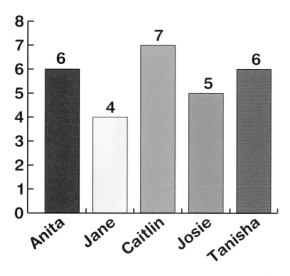

The Language of Statistics

Range, *median*, *mode*, and *mean* are the basic vocabulary of statistics.

RANGE

Range is the difference between the greatest and least number in a set of data.

	Minutes	Free Throws	Fouls	Points
Anita	25	6	3	12
Jane	14	4	3	8
Caitlin	22	7	4	16
Josie	19	5	2	14
Tanisha	30	6	5	21
Range	16	3	3	13

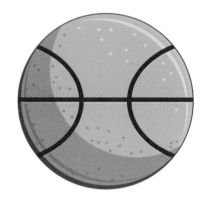

MEDIAN

Median is the middle number in a set of data. To find the median, arrange the numbers in order from least to greatest. The number in the middle is the *median*.

	Minutes
Tanisha	30
Anita	25
Caitlin	22
Josie	19
Jane	14

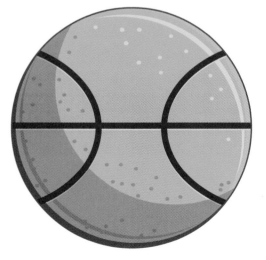

> **In an even-numbered set of data, the median is sometimes expressed as both middle numbers and sometimes as the average of the two middle numbers.**

MODE

Mode is the number that appears most often in a set of data. Some sets of data have no mode. Other sets have two or more modes.

	Minutes	Free Throws	Fouls	Points
Anita	25	6	3	12
Jane	14	4	3	8
Caitlin	22	7	4	16
Josie	19	5	2	14
Tanisha	30	6	5	21
Mode		6	3	

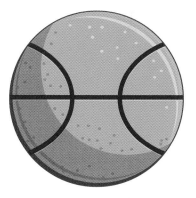

MEAN

Mean is the average number in a set of data (see Averages, p. 54).

	Minutes	Free Throws	Fouls	Points
Anita	25	6	3	12
Jane	14	4	3	8
Caitlin	22	7	4	16
Josie	19	5	2	14
Tanisha	30	6	5	21
Mean	22	5.6	3.4	14.2

Probability

What Is Probability?

Probability means the chance or likelihood that something will happen. In math, probability is a number that is used to describe that chance. The number is always between zero and one. **Zero** means **zero chance** that something will happen. **One** means that **something is certain to happen**. The closer the probability is to 1, the greater the chance that something will happen.

If you toss a coin, one of two things will result: heads or tails. Both a result of heads and a result of tails are possible, so the probability is **greater than zero**. But a result of heads is not certain, so the probability is **less than one**. In fact, the probability that heads will come up is one in two, or 1:2.

The Language of Probability

Probability is expressed in one of two ways: in **ratios** or **percentages** (see Ratios and Percentages, pages 50–51).

one in two chance of tossing heads = 1:2 or 50%

one in four chance of drawing the red ball = 1:4 or 25%

one in six chance of rolling the five = 1:6 or 16.7%

The Gambler's Dilemma: Probability and Statistics in Action

If you toss a coin, the probability of it coming up heads is *1:2*. In gambler's terms, heads is a *50/50* bet. (The term *50/50* means *50%* probability.) You have as much chance of winning with heads as you do with tails in all single tosses of the coin.

BIG LOSER

Say you've bet heads on fifty coin tosses, but each time the coin has come up tails.What is the probability that heads will come up on the fifty-first toss? The probability doesn't change, no matter how many times you toss the coin. Each coin toss has a 1:2 probability of coming up heads.

WHY THE DILEMMA?

Many people believe their chances of tossing heads improves after a long string of tossing tails. In fact, the chance of the coin landing heads up is no greater than it was on the first toss, 1:2, or 50%. But this belief illustrates the difference between probability and statistics.

Statistics are sometimes confused with probability, creating the gambler's dilemma. Toss a coin fifty times. Write down each result by noting the number of times heads came up in the fifty tosses. Then examine your data. Compare the number of times you got heads to the median number for fifty— twenty-five. Then compare your results to the mean number for fifty—also twenty-five. Both the mean and median numbers suggest that heads should come up twenty-five times.

Back to the unhappy gambler. Fifty coin tosses have not produced a heads result. Statistics suggest that heads should have come up twenty-five times. But probability for heads in any one toss of the coin remains *1:2*.

Remember, statistics and probability are different things. You can bet on it!

Chapter 1 The Abacus

Long before calculators and computers, people counted on the **_abacus_**. The abacus is a simple arithmetic machine built during the Chinese Sung dynasty (A.D. 960–1279). The abacus greatly increased the speed with which people could solve arithmetic problems.

The abacus soon became popular throughout the world. Students, as well as scientists, mathematicians, and merchants, learned to calculate on this marvelous machine.

The abacus consists of nine rows of beads strung on a framework of parallel wires. The beads are separated by a crossbar, forming two sections called "heaven" and "earth." There are two beads in each column of heaven. Each bead in heaven has a value of five. There are five beads in each column of earth. Each bead in earth has a value of **_1_**. Each column of beads has a value that increases by a power of **_10_**—just like our decimal system.

Calculators

Chapter 2 Simple Calculators

Early Calculators

Blaise Pascal (1623–1662) was a French mathematician and scientist. In 1642, at age 19, he invented the first calculator for adding and subtracting. Unlike the abacus, Pascal's calculator was very expensive and difficult to make. It never caught on. Then in 1671, Gottfried Wilhelm Leibniz invented a calculator that could multiply and divide numbers. Leibniz's machine was also expensive and complicated. Like Pascal's calculator, it never caught on.

Charles Babbage (1792–1871) began work in 1823 on a calculating machine that would solve arithmetic problems and then print out the answers. The machine was run with gear wheels. It was slow. It was so complicated that Babbage died before he finished building it.

Modern Calculators

During the twentieth century, calculators, which are really mini computers, were finally invented.

Calculators vary in design and in the kinds of problems they can solve.

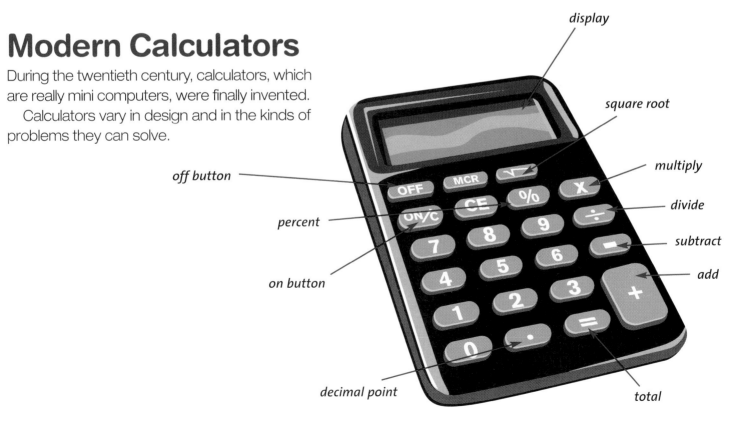

display

square root

multiply

divide

subtract

add

off button

percent

on button

decimal point

total

The Computer

The First Computers

The first electronic computers were built in the early 1900s. They were used mostly in wartime to break enemy codes.

Computers were enormous, expensive machines. They had to be kept in very large, refrigerated rooms. They were sold mostly to governments and businesses and were much too big and expensive for home use.

In the 1960s, transistors were invented and used to build computers. Transistors helped scientists reduce the size of the old giant computers.

When transistors were packed on chips, the computer revolution began.

Modern Computers

Computers today come in three basic kinds: **mainframe**, **mini**, and **micro**. The computers we have in our homes are microcomputers. Although mainframe, mini-, and microcomputers look very different, they are all programmable information-processing systems.

"Programmable" means that the computer can be told to follow sets of instructions, called **programs**. Once the computer is programmed, it will follow the instructions, or process the information in the program. **System** means a set of separate **components**, or items, that work together to process data.

Software

The instructions given to the computer are called **software**. Software is written on one of many high-level languages, such as BASIC, COBOL, C, and C++. A compiler or interpreter translates the program language into the **binary code**, or machine language.

monitor

keyboard

floppy disc drive

CD-ROM drive

CPU

mouse pad

mouse

Hardware

The processing components of a computer are called the **hardware**. The hardware includes internal memory, the central processing unit, or CPU, storage devices, and input/output devices.

The basic part of both internal memory and the CPU are **semiconductor chips**. These chips are tiny integrated electrical circuits. The circuits on the chips are either "on" or "off." "On" is 1 and "off" is 0 in base 2, or the **binary system** (see Base 2, p. 19). All instructions and data are encoded in the binary system for processing by the CPU. The alphabet, words, and numbers are also encoded in base 2.

Internal memory stores the instructions, or programs, as well as data, on chips. Internal memory is either random access memory (RAM) or read-only memory (ROM).

The CPU carries out, or processes, the instructions given in programs. The CPU follows the instructions stored in internal memory to process the data, which is also stored in internal memory. Chips are used in the CPU to process data.

Storage devices include external memory devices such as hard drives, floppy disks, CD-ROM disks, DVDs, MP3 players, and magnetic tapes. Input devices include keyboards, scanners, joysticks, and mice. Output devices include visual display units, or VDUs, printers, and modems.

The Internet and the World Wide Web

Groups of computers can be connected to each other to form a **network**, or **Internet**. This allows computers to "share" information with computers across town, across the country, or across the globe. The **World Wide Web** is a part of the Internet that allows different computer systems to share information by creating links between them.

The idea of an Internet connected by links in a World Wide Web has been around for several years. More than thirty years ago, a research and education system called ARPA (Advanced Research Projects Agency) successfully linked four U.S. universities. E-mail was introduced by 1972 and, in 1973, a standard for computer communications was designed. This standard was adopted in 1983 for the Internet design we use today.

Since the early 1980s, personal computers have become common household items. Since the late 1990s, most personal computer users have also become Internet users through the World Wide Web.

Glossary

absolute value The distance of a positive or negative number from 0. Absolute value is always stated as a positive number. (p. 10)

angle Formed by two rays with a common endpoint, called a vertex (p. 98), angles are measured in degrees from 0 to 180 and can be acute, obtuse, right, reflex, complementary, or supplementary. (pp. 99–100)

area The size of a flat surface in square units. (pp. 74 and 76)

circle A set of points within a plane where all points on the circle are at the same distance from a common point inside the circle, called the center. (p. 105)

counting numbers The set of natural numbers, beginning with 1 and continuing on to infinity. (p. 7)

decimal Fraction with a denominator of 10 or a power of 10. (p. 46)

decimal system System of numerals using tens symbols: 0, 1, 2, 3, 4, 5, 6, 7, 8, and 9. (p. 6)

factors Numbers that, when multiplied together, form a new number called a product. (p. 22)

fraction A number that represents a part of a whole. (p. 40)

graph A kind of drawing or diagram that shows data, or information, usually in numbers. (p. 114)

infinity The set of counting numbers that has no end. (p. 7)

integers The set of numbers that includes counting numbers, zero, and whole numbers less than zero. (p. 9)

line Made up of points that extend in opposite directions and go on without end. (p. 94)

multiples Numbers that can be multiplied together to make a common product. (p. 23)

order of operations The order in which mathematical functions, such as addition or division, are carried out in a math problem. Perform all operations in parentheses first, followed by exponents, multiplication and division and, finally, addition and subtraction. (p. 57)

percentage A ratio written as a decimal fraction. The term percent means "part per hundred." (p. 50)

perimeter The distance around a polygon. (p. 74)

points Locator marks used to tell the position of lines and objects. Points have no sizes or dimensions, that is, they have no width, length, or height. (p. 93)

polygon Two-dimensional, or flat, shapes formed from three or more line segments that lie within one plane. (p. 101)

power The product of a number multiplied by itself many times. The first power of a number is the number itself. The second power is the number multiplied once by itself, the third power is the number multiplied twice by itself, etc. Powers are expressed in exponents, tiny numbers written above and to the right of the number. (p. 24)

properties Laws or characteristics of addition and multiplication. (pp. 56–57)

ratio A way to describe things by comparing them to each other. A ratio can be written in the form of a fraction (for example, ½) or using a colon (for example, 1:2) to separate the two items being compared. (p. 50)

set A collection of items, for example, coins, marbles, dishes, trading cards, or even numbers. (p. 12)

volume The amount of space contained in a three-dimensional space figure—usually length, width, and height—and measured in cubic units. (p. 77)

Index

Notes

Notes

Notes

Notes

Notes

Notes

Notes